THE
MOUNTAIN BIKE
EXPERIENCE

A Complete Introduction to the Joys of Off-Road Riding

AN OWL BOOK
HENRY HOLT AND COMPANY
NEW YORK

THE
MOUNTAIN BIKE
EXPERIENCE

Dave King
and Michael Kaminer

Henry Holt and Company, Inc.
Publishers since 1866
115 West 18th Street
New York, New York 10011

Henry Holt® is a registered
trademark of Henry Holt and Company, Inc.

LIBRARY OF CONGRESS CATALOGING-IN-PUBLICATION DATA
King, Dave.
The mountain bike experience: a complete introduction to the joys
of off-road riding/Dave King and Michael Kaminer.—1st ed.
p.   cm.
"An owl book."
Includes bibliographical references and index.
1. All-terrain cycling. I. Kaminer, Michael. II. Title.
GV1056.K56   1996   95-37734
796.6'4—dc20   CIP

ISBN 0-8050-3723-3

Henry Holt books are available for special promotions and premiums.
For details contact: Director, Special Markets.

First Edition—1996

Illustrations © 1996 by Steve Vanderbosch
Designed by Kathryn Parise

Printed in the United States of America
All first editions are printed on acid-free paper. ∞

1   3   5   7   9   10   8   6   4   2

To Scott

CONTENTS

■ ■ ■ ■ ■

ACKNOWLEDGMENTS

The authors would like to express their gratitude to
Mount Snow, Vermont, the National Off-Road Bicycle Association,
and the International Mountain Bicycling Association for their tireless work
in promoting the sport of mountain biking. Special appreciation goes
to the millions of mountain bikers across the United States,
without whom this book would not have been possible.

THE
MOUNTAIN BIKE
EXPERIENCE

INTRODUCTION

· · · · ·

VERMONT MAN'S SHOCKING CONFESSION:
"Mountain Biking Changed My Life"

Most people who have undergone a radical transformation in life can recall the exact moment it happened. Mine came on a freezing December night fifteen years ago. At the time, I was living in West Dover, Vermont, and working as a chef. One Sunday, my day off, I watched television and ate continuously—my favorite hobbies at the time. Outside, snow started falling and soon built up into one of those blinding blizzards that make you wish you'd never left the womb. By nighttime, the storm had ended, and the snow looked so beautiful that I wanted to play in my backyard. As a teenager I'd loved snowshoeing; though I hadn't tried it since, I couldn't resist now.

There was just one difference, though. At age twenty-four, I carried a gargantuan 265 pounds—and a forty-two-inch waist—on a six-foot frame. It made any kind of physical activity, even walking, an ordeal. I hated my body, but as a chef I wrote it off as an occupational hazard. To console myself, I even rationalized that being fat boosted my professional credibility.

Defying common sense, I bundled up, carefully tied on my snowshoes, and stepped into a slashing wind. After trudging about fifty feet, I started gasping uncontrollably. My legs felt liquid, and I thought I would heave my insides. Either by instinct or by providence, I found my way back to the house.

For a few days, I was so sore that I felt like I'd been hit by a truck—just from a short walk. At first the whole experience disturbed and frightened me; after a while, the fear began motivating me. Unless I changed my lifestyle, it would eventually kill me. And change I did, with a vengeance.

First, I began changing the way I thought about food. After doing some research on nutrition, I used my culinary skills to design a low-fat, high-carbohydrate diet. I followed it with religious ardor and lost eighty pounds within three months. I also discovered exercise for the first time in my life. A friend who had lost a hundred pounds himself suggested the *Canadian Air Force Training Manual,* which contains a progressive fitness regimen that carries you through an entire two-year program.

By the time I completed the plan, I was running fifty miles a week—quite an achievement for someone who hadn't touched his toes in twenty years. About a year later, I got a job teaching Nautilus and free weights at a gym, surprising myself and everyone I knew. Being athletic was still a novelty, and I almost felt I had to prove that my renovated self could prevail over the old one.

At the time, I still ran to keep in shape. But the monotonous clip-clopping of running started getting to me. I'd heard that cycling offered some of the same physical benefits, so I dropped in on a Brattleboro bike shop to investigate. Flipping through a catalog of new bikes coming out that year, I saw a boring bunch of racing and touring bikes. Then, a revelation: the catalog presented a weird-looking bike with fat tires and flat handlebars that looked like an old 1950s balloon-tired Schwinn.

The clerk explained that it was a mountain bike. It was versatile enough, he said, to handle hard hills, dirt roads, trails, whatever. It was love at first sight. I could tell that this bike would provide my ticket out of exercise ennui. Without hesitating, I ordered one. A week later, I plunked down $450 and became the proud owner of one of the first Specialized Stumpjumpers, the progenitor of today's mountain bikes.

1

ZEN AND THE ART OF MOUNTAIN BIKING

A Holistic Approach to Overcoming Obstacles

Q: What did the Buddhist monk say to the hot dog vendor?
A: "Make me one with everything."

In my fifteen years as a mountain biker and instructor, I've discovered what really limits beginners once they hit the trail. It's not flab, or bunions, or the fact that they haven't traveled on fewer than four wheels since 1972. It's attitude. The expectations you bring to the trail, and your outlook while you ride, mean more to the mountain biking experience than physical shape. They can, in fact, make the difference between biking nirvana and hell on wheels.

Before they ever hit a trail, most people bring what I call an adversarial approach to both their bike and the terrain. They see steep hills and calculate how quickly they can conquer them. They want to control the bike's every tire squeal. Soon, they begin imagining a conspiracy among rocks, logs, and other inanimate objects to make their ride as miserable as possible.

Relax, folks. Trees and rocks probably have nothing against you, and they were there before you, anyway. Stop thinking of terrain as hostile. Rethinking your instinctive approach to obstacles is the first step to making mountain biking more enjoyable—and a lot less stressful. Obstacles, in fact, represent opportunities in mountain biking. Every rock, every log, every hill offers a chance to better your skills and broaden your experience. If you can adopt that frame of mind, you can transform the riding experience from an endurance test into an exhilarating succession of challenges. You'll also learn a lot more.

Later in the book, I'll go over the particular body positions that work best in different riding situations. But first, I want to share what I've discovered about the psychological aspect of riding. The more you ride, the more you'll

learn that successful mountain biking is equal parts physical law and mental attitudes.

To begin with, your riding experience will at first feel like an epic battle between you and your intuition. Most people tend to think of intuition as a magical power, an absolute that's always correct. To me, it means a fluid framework you apply to life based on your experiences. Once your experience changes, your intuitiveness changes as well. If you let intuition steer you on the trail, it becomes a prejudice, a self-fulfilling prophecy. Blindly following it means you've already made up your mind. If intuition nags that you're going to hit that rock and log ahead and crash, you'll want to avoid the situation altogether. If it complains you're going to get muddy sloshing through that puddle up ahead, you'll probably interrupt your ride to avoid that, too.

Wipe the slate clean. Unlearn your intuition on the trail. I still have to consciously push mine away; after thousands of hours on my bike, my gut will still tell me I can't handle an especially gnarly trail. But with experience, you learn to rethink. And you find the harmony that's halfway between freedom and fear. Soon, instead of wishing rocks and trees would disappear, you may start wishing there were more of them.

To begin with, hitting the trail in attack mode will drain you and exhaust your resources almost instantaneously. When you reach a hill or a steep incline, for example, don't worry about making it to the top. You'll push too hard and tire yourself in a short burst. Instead, pull your thoughts back into yourself and your bike. Try to focus on the process behind what you're doing. Concentrate on every

single pedal stroke, striving to make each one perfect and complete. Don't try to beat the hill, because you won't. Develop a steady cadence and see how slowly you can get to the top, instead.

Obviously, you won't break any land speed records this way. Speed shouldn't be your object, in the first place. You will, however, probably make it to the top of hills you thought you couldn't climb—without hating life itself by the time you reach the top. As they climb hills, most people will also fix their longing eyes on the horizon, as if this might draw it closer. This can make a slight incline feel like one of the Tetons. Instead, pay attention to the terrain right in front of you. By not constantly reminding yourself how far you have to go, you can shift your focus away from the hill and into yourself.

Take a similar approach riding downhill. Don't fight the terrain; try not to steer your bike. The bicycle knows the route it wants to follow—its path of least resistance—so let it do what it wants. While this might sound like a mystical pronouncement, it's actually just rudimentary physics. When I teach a beginner's class how to ride downhill, I tell them to imagine emptying a fifty-gallon vat of water down the hill, and visualize where the water would flow. Your bike will "flow" the same way. When you reach the top of a hill, try that mental exercise. Then let yourself relax and allow the bike to travel where it feels it should. Direct it, of course, but don't dominate it. Rather than influence its direction, concentrate on navigating the terrain. By not trying to control the bike, you'll be able to control it.

If you start riding with friends, and most

people do, you'll have to overcome another instinct: protecting your ego. From the day you start, you'll always see people better than you. You have to learn to accept their skill and embrace your own limitations. Once you recognize your own strengths and weaknesses, you can achieve self-awareness. Don't fight your limits; accentuate your strengths. If you're older, don't beat your head against the wall because you've lost strength or agility. You've probably gained endurance.

Don't lament what you don't have; use what you do. You'll help reach that self-awareness by ignoring the one-dimensional media image of mountain biking. To sell itself, the sport has been promoted as an aggressive, testosterone-driven frenzy. You wouldn't know it from some of the printed material and videos, but there's a place within the sport for everyone. All it takes is a bike and a place to ride it. If you're open to it, self-discovery starts with the first pedal stroke. Set your priorities and learn what needs work.

Once you accept your limitations, stop lambasting yourself for what you can't do and don't let your expectations get out of control. Some things may never become easy, so accept that and move on to what's next. Off the mountain bike, I'm sure there are a million things you can do that the next person can't. Watch someone who can do something better and learn from him or her. I like to tell new students about a woman who walked through the door at the mountain biking school one Saturday morning a few years ago—with a cane. No one said a word when we saw her, but every instructor's eyes screamed, "Oh my God, what if I get her in my class?"

For me, though, it presented an incredible teaching opportunity. How gutsy to leave her ego behind for this experience, I thought. I couldn't wait to join her on the trail, to help her fulfill whatever goals she had for herself. She, in turn, was thrilled just to get on a bike again. A week after she left, I got one of the most inspiring letters I've ever read in my life. "You've shown me nothing's impossible," she wrote. "You let me experience something I never thought I could."

Anyone can achieve that sense of accomplishment on different levels. Her experience wobbling down a tiny trail feels identical to mine thrashing down the gnarliest thing in the world. Challenging yourself at the appropriate level, and being honest about your goals, will bring fulfillment on your own terms. That's what matters. It takes patience, and often failure, to discover strengths and weaknesses. So enjoy the process. Don't fear change. What's the worst that can happen?

That's what I had to convince another memorable student—a rabbi. He'd obviously spent a lot of life studying and learning. My impression was that he'd spent much of his life exploring the experiences of others, and that this was his first chance to fully inhabit his own. When I explained that so much of riding came down to personal preference, he looked very nervous; I think he had hoped for connect-the-dots instructions.

Over the course of a weekend, we pushed him little by little. Cautious and deliberate at first, he began opening up. By the end of the weekend, he was first in line to ride forty feet from the top of a sand pile into a huge puddle, whooping and screaming all the way down. In

the process, he'd rediscovered a part of himself that he'd buried. (Three years later at a Manhattan bike shop, an acquaintance behind the counter told me about a little guy who'd bought a bike and said the mountain biking weekend was the experience of his lifetime. Mountain biking *can* change your perspective on life.)

Some people, of course, can't cope with any activity that's not closely regulated. Take the

case of the high-powered professional and self-described "control freak" who micromanaged the trail to death her first day out. Every pebble generated a reaction way out of proportion to what it deserved. I spent the whole weekend trying to convince her to ignore little things. I explained that micromanaging chops your ride into a series of specific issues instead of a smooth continuum. It sucks out the flow of riding until you become acutely conscious of each component of the ride, which is exactly the opposite of what it should feel like.

The next day, when she finally started listening and letting go, she had an amazing breakthrough. She began overlooking little nuisances instead of overreacting to terrain. And once she did, she began enjoying a completely different experience. Little by little, she discovered that she would survive taking chances, so the chances she took got bigger. To her relief, she didn't fly over handles when she rode over stones or have her flesh ripped by stray branches.

She kept pretty quiet about her progress until Sunday night, when she and her husband started packing their car. But once we began reminiscing about the weekend, she confessed how much micromanaging had become a major issue in her life—and how the biking experience had helped her confront it for the first time. "It finally hit me," she told us, "sometimes I just need to float over details and let them happen." I always like to say, mountain biking makes great therapy—and it's a lot more fun than lying on a couch.

On the other hand, some students refuse to take any initiative. They see instructors as gurus; they think we have all the answers. In fact, I think of myself as a supplier of questions. I'd rather give information that starts a process rather than ends one. And that process is endless no matter what your skill level or experience. When you approach instruction and learning that way, you create independent people, not dependent pupils.

There was an incredible learning curve at the beginning of my biking life. I experienced one breakthrough after another, from the

mundane ("Now I know how to jump a log") to the sublime ("Like, I'm riding where dinosaurs once walked"). I try to convey the same kind of experience to new riders. Rather than read this book for steps A, B, and C, let it guide you as you learn to fail and fall, accept taking risks, and gain an awareness of yourself beyond biking. My highest goal as an instructor is to get people to connect with that experience and learn for themselves what they can accomplish.

To inspire you (I hope) as you pedal your way to nirvana, I've come up with my own loose guidelines. I usually rebel against anything that smacks of dogma, so I don't want to create a set of rules for mountain biking. Just apply these to your own experiences as you develop your own style:

1. Mountain biking is not a series of obstacles, but a succession of opportunities. Every rock, every log, every hill offers an opportunity to better your skills and broaden your experience.

2. Attitude, not ability, sets your limits. Thinking that you're not an athlete can stop you from becoming one. Change your attitude and you discover a new self.

3. Let your bike follow the path of least resistance. Gravity determines where the bike travels, so don't fight it. Imagine where water would flow if you poured it down the trail. Work with natural forces to direct yourself and guide your bike.

4. Trust your bike and trust yourself. Learn to communicate with your bike and understand the signals it sends. And learn to appreciate yourself enough to learn from both positive and negative experiences.

5. Expectations create reality. If you think you'll fall, you will. If you think you can climb mountains, you will.

6. Respect your natural neighborhood. A mountain bike connects you to your surroundings in a new way. It provides a fresh perspective on your environment. Once you understand where you are, respect will follow.

7. In mountain biking, the means is the end. The process is the goal. Mountain biking is much like skiing; it's not about getting down the hill, but what happens along the way. Enjoy the ride.

8. Mountain biking is risk management. Once you learn to overcome the risks involved, you'll feel more confident about accepting bigger challenges in life.

9. Adversity isn't negative. Rather, it teaches persistence and patience. It gives insight into the whole riding experience. Learn from bad rides or bad days. Enrich and challenge yourself.

10. Wherever you want to go, mountain bikes will take you. Use your bike as a vehicle for any kind of experience, from self-improvement to self-discovery, from exploring the backcountry to navigating your neighborhood.

From a technical standpoint, I could list all the required skills for mountain biking, but you can't really separate them. All aspects of riding constitute parts of a whole. What you're doing at any given moment results directly from what's under your tires. Think of it as a dance, with the terrain as your choreographer. Feel the riding surface through the tires, the fork, the frame. The bike becomes an extension of your body. You are connected to the bike, the bike feeds you information from the trail, and you react and speak back to the bike, telling it what to do to negotiate a particular section of trail. Listen to what the bike tells you and respond quickly and appropriately.

I love the feeling of connectedness, of an almost Zen unity, with my surroundings. Every part of the experience relates to every other part. Taking that kind of holistic approach enriches your riding experience. The fact that 10,000 years ago a glacier left rocks on the trail near my home in Dover, Vermont, is important. Instead of just riding over rocks, you begin to realize why those rocks are there. Instead of just thinking you're out in the middle of nowhere, you begin realizing you're actually riding over ages-old terrain with a million years' worth of stories.

The environment has a rich history, and mountain biking lets you explore it by fostering an interaction between you as an individual and the planet. Understanding that history brings respect and increases your enjoyment. In that sense, mountain biking can also become a vehicle for the natural and the spiritual worlds because it connects you with another time. More than once, I've tried to imagine the prehistoric landscape of Dover. And sometimes, I feel I can see the distant past in the rocks strewn and scraped by glaciers.

One trail I often ride was once the main road between Dover and Wardsboro, Vermont, many years ago. Deep into this trail, in what feels like the middle of nowhere, stands a memorial to a man gored and killed by a bull on his way back from the Dover Fair in 1858. A fist clutching a broken chain is engraved in a huge stone. You can't help but imagine the whole scene of 150 years ago. Was this poor guy walking his bull home from Dover? How did these people live?

Most of the time in modern society there's no such sense of continuity, no consciousness of history. So much of who we are, the patterns of our daily lives, relate back to people and events from the past, especially in small towns. It sounds romantic, but you gain a real, direct relationship to these events. We tend to think the past is irrelevant. Where I live, that's not true. From a century ago, settlers' roads determine where mountain biking trails go today. For me, the circle of past and present keeps getting wider.

Mountain biking also lets you look at things without preconceptions. It takes you out into the wilderness and disconnects you from human influence. It's just you and the land and the bike—nothing else is there because a person put it there. You're taking the experience back to its primal elements. Every experience on the trail is valid. It's a question of individual receptivity rather than anything inherent in the experience itself. So open yourself.

To help you get there, I'd like to offer this highly spiritual piece of wisdom: get off your bike. Lean it against a tree, take a hike. Look for signs of wildlife, identify plants, observe nature. Dismounting is as integral a part of the riding experience as riding itself. Too many new riders become compulsive about main taining perpetual motion for hours. Why limit yourself that way? Your bike is, ultimately, a vehicle, and its function is to get you someplace. Ideally it should disappear from beneath you. Your bike is the means to an end. While the act of riding is a complete experience, using your bike to go somewhere for another experience gives you both the means *and* the end—a completeness.

On a mountain bike, your history and the place's history converge in the now. Being involved in the process of riding, you just always want to stay in the here. Then you get to the next here, and the here after that, and your destination is the final here. It's like the aging process. Set your goals and enjoy the process as you reach them. Experience the now and enjoy it.

2

......

YOUR MOUNTAIN BIKE, YOURSELF

Bicycle Anatomy and Maintenance

Don't let all the metaphysical talk fool you. I'm really interested in your body, and I'd like to explore it with you. In fact, becoming familiar with the body of your bike is just as important—if not more important—as knowing how to ride it.

Your mountain bike can perform as an extension of your body. It can disappear from under you when you reach the perfect riding place, where everything comes together and you know you're in the groove. But it's essential that your bike perform at its best to get you there. A good working knowledge of your bike can also make the difference between walking or riding back to civilization when something goes awry. Recognizing what's fixable and what's not can save you a lot of time; you won't waste valuable daylight desperately trying in vain to repair some mangled part.

A chef couldn't cook a soufflé without understanding which ingredients make it rise; likewise, understanding the basic operations of a bike will help you adapt to anything out of the ordinary. Picture this scene: A stick gets caught in your rear derailleur and spokes. Two spokes break, and the derailleur, while not broken, doesn't function. By knowing how these components operate, you'll be able to analyze what's not working properly and either fix it or adapt its configuration so you can ride the bike. How far you go with maintenance and repair is up to you. Many of the maintenance tasks in this chapter require special tools and experience. When in doubt, consult a qualified bike mechanic. In the long run, you'll save both time and money.

In this chapter, I'll try to familiarize you with basic concepts of bike anatomy and function. An entire book could be written on the subject, and many have; if one of your goals is to be able to take your bike apart and put it back together in the dark, I suggest you consult one of the many excellent bicycle maintenance books available at your local bookstore.

The most important tool to bring on the trail is your brain. Serious riding means you'll need imagination and creativity to solve problems that can't be anticipated. You can do it by understanding your bike. There's only so much you can do to be prepared out on the trail. In chapter 4 we talk about what you need to fix the most common problems trailside.

To me, one of the most beautiful things about a bicycle is its simplicity of design. We've seen a lot of innovations in mountain biking over the last few years—essential breakthroughs that raised the sport to a new height (suspension and clipless pedals come to mind). But nothing compares to a bare-bones, stripped-down ultralight racer. In it, I see beauty in its purest form—the beauty of functionality.

Superficially, not much seems to separate

today's mountain bike from bikes of fifty, or even a hundred, years ago. Same two wheels, same chain drive. But there's been a revolution in bicycle technology, spawned largely by the success of mountain biking itself. It's been a revolution of frame materials and component design. Innovations have come so fast over the last ten years it's almost annoying. Just when you get comfortable with one design, along comes a better one. Back in the mid- to late eighties, we saw so many changes from year to year that it became impossible to guess what would turn up on your next visit to the bike shop. Problem is, although an innovation sounds better or looks better, it ain't necessarily so. While many innovations still see the light of day, I'm happy to report that the era of flash-in-the-pan fads seems to have ended.

This chapter describes the bike and all (or most) of its parts; it also offers guidelines for routine maintenance as well as insights into the relationships between all these parts and how they affect the riding experience.

Physically the bike can be divided into seven basic systems:

1. The bearings
2. The drive train
3. The frame
4. The steer mechanism
5. The suspension assembly
6. The brake assembly
7. The wheels

1. THE BEARINGS

Bearings are designed to cut down on friction between moving parts on a bike. Bearing assemblies are part of the wheel hubs, the bottom bracket, the headset, and the pedal spindles. The principles of function and adjustment in all of these parts are nearly identical.

Bearings roll on bearing races. Races are doughnut-shaped concave indentations made to fit the corresponding bearings precisely and are found on the spindle (whether it's the crown race found on the steer tube, the bottom bracket spindle, the wheel axle, or the pedal spindle) and the bearing assembly (the headset, bottom bracket, wheel hub, or pedal). The smoothness of the races and the bearings,

Fig. 2.1: Bottom bracket assembly
a. adjustable cup; b. fixed cup; c. bottom bracket spindle; d. bearing housing
(Photo by Mike Piniewski)

combined with good, old-fashioned grease, makes for virtually friction-free operation (when properly adjusted) of these key points on your bike.

You'll know your bearings are adjusted perfectly when they slide on the races freely when the spindle is turned but don't have excessive play. Look at Figure 2.1; using the bottom bracket as an example, you can see an adjusting cup and a fixed cup in the bottom bracket assembly. You can adjust the bottom bracket by varying the tightness of the adjustable cup; the tighter the adjustment, the more the adjustable cup squeezes the spindle and bearings against the fixed cup. The adjustment is perfect when the spindle turns freely but there is no looseness in the bearings. After you've gotten the adjustment just right, lock it in place with the locking nut. Loose bearings will knock around inside the bearing assembly and will eventually damage the races, pitting them and making it impossible to adjust the bottom bracket properly. Each bearing assembly found on your bike has the same basic parts and is adjusted the same way. Recent developments such as cartridge bottom brackets and sealed bearing headsets eliminate the need for routine adjustment, making the bike easier to maintain.

MAINTENANCE: Keeping bearings properly adjusted is really your only maintenance chore. If you ride a lot, or in very wet conditions, and have conventional bearing assemblies, you may want your local shop to lube your bottom bracket, headset, and wheel bearings a couple of times a year.

2. THE DRIVE TRAIN

The drive train is the sum of all parts related to the propulsion of the bike. This includes the **pedals, crank arms, bottom bracket, chain rings, rear gear cluster, chain, front and rear derailleurs** and **gear shift levers,** and the **freehub or freewheel** (see Figure 2.2).

You activate the drive train by pushing your feet down on the pedals, which turns the crank arms, which in turn rotate the front chain rings. The chain rings turn the chain, which drives the rear cog, which is attached to the rear hub, causing the rear wheel to turn forward, propelling the bike.

The drive train has the majority of a bike's moving parts. Since these parts stay close to the ground (most of the time) and are largely unprotected from the elements, the drive train tends to get very dirty. It needs regular cleaning and maintenance.

Pedals fall into two groups: conventional and clipless. For six years I rode my bike with old-fashioned bear-trap pedals, wearing twenty-pound, size 13EEE hiking boots with no toe clips. Toe clips were for road bikes; you couldn't use them on a mountain bike because they'd prevent you from sticking your foot out to prevent a fall (*dabbing,* in mountain bike vernacular).

I was sure it would always be so, and swore that you just could not ride ultratechnical Vermont terrain with toe clips (when we use the word *technical* in reference to terrain we're talking about trails with rocks, logs, loose gravel, or anything that will require good mountain bike riding *technique* to negotiate). I was wrong. In fact, when I finally found some clips and straps that would accept my huge feet in 1988, it changed my riding forever—for the better.

My other pedal epiphany came when I first rode clipless pedals in 1990. After an initial tip-over-at-slow-speeds stage, I discovered a new kind of security on the trail. Gone were the boots big enough to hold a keg of beer; in their place came somewhat less massive shoes. That meant an instant power transfer from shoe to cranks. No more flipping the pedal with my toe to get my foot in. Wow!

Clipless pedals are really a complete system that incorporates the shoe, the cleat, and the pedal. Mountain bike clipless pedals differ from road clipless in that they are double sided, so you don't have to bother flipping the pedal over with your toe to get in; you just put your foot down and clip in. There are lots of different clipless systems out there, and by the time this book goes to press there'll be more, but most operate on a spring tension mechanism that holds the cleat in place until it's twisted laterally.

The most important thing to know about

Fig. 2.2: The drive train
a. pedals; b. crank arm; c. bottom bracket; d. chain rings; e. chain; f. rear gear cluster;
g. front and rear derailleurs *(Photo by Mike Piniewski)*

pedals is that they *tighten* to the front and *loosen* to the rear. Pedals are designed this way so that the act of pedaling will tend to tighten both pedals. In other words, one pedal has reverse threads and the other doesn't. It doesn't really matter which is which; just remember that when you want to loosen a pedal, turn the pedal wrench toward the back of the bike. When you want to tighten it, turn it toward the front. I've seen pedal threads stripped beyond repair by people employing serious leverage to loosen a pedal, when all along it was being tightened.

MAINTENANCE:
Standard pedals with clips and straps: There's not a lot to do to pedals except to keep an eye on the spindle bearings to make sure they're not too worn. It's generally smarter to replace your pedals than to try to rebuild the bearings, and in many low-end pedals you can't get inside the bearing assembly, anyway.

Clipless pedals: Keep the release mechanism as clean as possible, and lube occasionally with a Teflon-based spray. Since clipless pedals tend to be so expensive, it may be worthwhile to repack the bearings if they get worn. It's not easy, though; you need to replace the spindle, and the bearings in a pedal are tiny and easy to lose.

Crank arms are levers, and as we learned in high school physics, the longer the lever, the more force is exerted on its fulcrum (in this case, the bottom bracket spindle). The most common crank length on mountain bikes is 175 mm, although 170-mm cranks can be found on smaller bikes. The shorter the crank the more clearance, but you trade off power and leverage. Smaller-frame bikes (usually 14- and 16-inch models) have shorter cranks, for two reasons. One, a small bike is closer to the ground and needs a shorter crank for adequate ground clearance. Second, a smaller person's legs aren't long enough to efficiently exert high torque at low rpms on a longer lever.

Road bikes tend to have shorter cranks because what matters is a relatively high cadence (100–120 rpm, as compared to 70–90 rpm for mountain biking). In road biking, spin is where it's at, and shorter cranks create a smaller circle of motion than longer cranks, allowing the legs to pump faster for the same amount of rotations of the bottom bracket. Mountain biking, on the other hand, requires low rpm maneuvers in the single track (a narrow, shoulder-width trail designed for foot or two-wheeled use, as opposed to double-track, or fire, roads, made for four-wheeled vehicles), which means you need maximum leverage.

MAINTENANCE: Crank arms can, on occasion, loosen. If your bottom bracket area creaks, it's probably because of loose cranks. Tighten them by using either a 14-mm socket wrench on older bikes, or an 8-mm Allen wrench on newer models. Although manufacturers specify torque values for cranks, it's usually enough to tighten them as much as possible without forcing.

The bottom bracket is the bearing assembly to which the crank arms attach. The bottom bracket provides a point on which cranks can turn. It consists of the bottom bracket spindle (the "axle" to which the crank arms bolt), the bearing assembly, and the housing, which is threaded on its outside circumference so that it may be secured on the corresponding threads of the bottom bracket tube in the frame.

In recent years, most mid- to high-end bikes have come outfitted with a cartridge-style bottom bracket. This means the spindle and bearing assemblies are manufactured as one sealed unit, which accomplishes two things. First, the sealed mechanism tends to keep out water and dirt; second, it virtually eliminates the need for adjustment. The old-style bottom bracket has parts that are, in comparison, much more exposed to the elements. More than once I've extricated a worn-out bottom bracket from my bike, and instead of bearings and grease, found brown water, rusty metal, and a ball of smelly sludge that used to be grease. Happily, cartridge bottom brackets have eliminated this problem.

MAINTENANCE: See maintenance for bearings (page 16).

The front chain rings and the rear gear cluster are the cogs on which the chain travels. The chain rings are part of the crank assembly; the term *crankset* includes the crank arms and the chain rings. Chain rings come in different sizes, expressed in the number of teeth on the individual ring. When reading the specs of a crankset, for example, the numbers 24, 36, 46 mean that the inner ring has 24 teeth, the middle ring 36, and the outer ring 46. The more teeth in a chain ring, the more revolutions of the rear wheel hub per pedal stroke and the faster the bike goes. Outer rings are the largest and are used for pedaling on a road or on a high-speed downhill. Middle rings are for level single-track or moderate climbs, and the inner or "granny" gear is used for steep climbing.

The rear gear cluster attaches to the rear hub. The chain, driven by the front chain rings, turns the rear cogs and rear hub, turning the rear wheel and propelling the bike. With each chain ring you have a range of gears to use in the rear. Most bikes now come with either 7- or 8-speed rear cogs. A "7-speed cassette" means there are seven cogs in the gear assembly, each one with a different number of teeth. Multiply the number of chain rings times the number of cogs in the rear cluster and that's how many speeds you have. Three up front times seven in the rear gives you twenty-one speeds.

A *gear ratio* refers to the relationship between the front and rear chain rings. A chain running on a 26-tooth front chain ring and a 26-tooth rear cog means a gear ratio of 1:1. Each time you turn the cranks one full revolution, the rear hub, and therefore the rear wheel, turns one revolution. When you have a 21-speed bike you have twenty-one different combinations, or ratios. There are complicated formulas for divining "gear inches," an arcane system of measuring gear ratios that goes back to the days when bikes had huge front and tiny rear wheels. There's no reason why you need to know any mathematical formulas. Eventually, you'll learn to select instinctively the proper, most comfortable gear for each riding situation. However, the history of gearing does help us understand some of the underlying concepts (see page 20).

These Victorian babies required a handlebar mustache (now you know where the term came from) and a ladder for mounting. Back then the only way to change the speed of a bike was to change the size of the wheel. There were no gears; the cranks were attached directly to the front hub. One turn of the cranks equaled one turn of the wheel. The bigger the wheel, the farther the bike traveled per pedal stroke. The big breakthrough came when someone figured out that a gear on the crank and a gear in the rear with a chain would equal the effect of a big wheel without actually having one. In other words, you were no longer trapped by the one-turn-of-the-cranks-equals-one-turn-of-the-pedals law; now you could design a faster bike where one turn of the pedals equaled three turns of the rear wheel. It was still just a 1-speed bike—derailleurs weren't invented for another forty years—but now almost anyone could ride, and the first big bicycle craze took off. By estimating gear inches, we're really estimating how big the wheel of one of these old bikes would have to be to match the gear you're using.

By moving the chain with the derailleurs you change the combination of gears front to back in response to changing terrain. You reach your biggest gear (highest, fastest) when your chain is on the biggest gear in the front and the smallest in the back. Your smallest gear (lowest, easiest) means your chain is on the smallest gear up front and the biggest in the rear. The higher the number of teeth up front—compared to the number in the rear—the more times the wheel turns per pedal stroke and the faster the bike will go. The higher the number of teeth in the rear, compared to the number in the front, the fewer times the wheel turns per pedal stroke— and the easier it becomes to go uphill.

Think of your gears as you would an automobile transmission. You are the car's engine. When the car is in first gear, the engine has to turn at relatively high rpm in order to move forward. As the car builds momentum, you shift so that the vehicle will move faster, but the engine still turns at approximately the same rate. This is precisely the way gearing on a bike works, but because the human engine can turn the pedals only so fast, there are many more gears on a bicycle than a car.

The chain is a series of links joined together by pins. Each tooth of the gears fits in between the links of the chain. Because of the improvements in gearing (like 8-speed cassettes) chains have also become relatively high-tech. Because of the necessity of putting cogs closer together to accommodate 8-speed cassettes, chains need to be narrow but strong.

MAINTENANCE: Keeping the whole shebang clean is probably the most important thing you can do for your gears. Excessive dirt and grit carried on the chain act as an abrasive on the gears and can wear them down. Use a Teflon-based dry lube, not oil, on your chain. Oil gets sticky and gunky and collects dust and grit, acting as a medium for the distribution of abrasive dirt throughout the drive train. Don't underlube your chain, as this can cause links to freeze and could possibly damage your derailleur. A good rule of thumb: lube the chain when it appears dry and sounds squeaky when you ride. With experience, you'll begin to *feel* when the chain needs lubing.

Your mechanic has specialized tools to diagnose worn-out rear cogs and chains. Worn rear cogs will cause the chain to skip when there is a heavy load (as in hill climbs) and, when the front gears wear, chain suck. Don't get too excited; *chain suck* is what happens when the chain is not released from the bottom of the chain ring as it travels toward the rear derailleur, dragging the chain up into the chain stays and jamming it between the chain rings and the chain stay. This usually happens to the granny gear first, and can be diagnosed by inspecting the granny gear carefully. If your gear is worn out, you'll see that the top of each tooth is hooked in the direction of rotation. These hooks are responsible for the chain's not being released. The only remedy for this is to replace the gear. Other problems can also cause chain suck (a mud-fouled chain, for instance), so check with your mechanic when these symptoms become chronic to avoid a Chain Suck Massacre.

The front and rear derailleurs, along with the **gear shift levers,** move the chain through the front and rear gears, giving the rider access to different gear combinations. The basic design, construction, and function of derailleurs are more or less the same front and back, with some exceptions. Each derailleur has a four-sided, hinged main body. When tension is applied to the shifter cable and its attachment on the derailleur, the shape of the derailleur body changes, moving the chain through the gears.

For such a critical part, the front derailleur is a fairly simple affair. When you want to shift to the next largest chain ring, you push the front shifter, which applies tension to the cable and then the front derailleur. The front derailleur cage nudges the chain and starts it moving toward the next gear.

The rear derailleur, however, is more complicated. Along with its function as a shifter, it acts as a chain tensioner. When the chain moves from one gear combination to the next, the amount of slack in the chain changes because of differences in the physical size of the gears. Too much slack in the chain will make it slip when you pedal. The rear derailleur accommodates for these changes by taking up the slack in the chain with the jockey pulleys and the pulley cage. A strong spring at the top of the pulley cage pulls the chain toward the rear of the bike, taking up the slack in the chain. At the same time, the derailleur moves the chain laterally to the bike, moving the chain from cog to cog.

Both front and rear derailleur have return springs that automatically move the derailleur toward the smaller gears. As you shift to the smaller cogs (remember, that's the lower gears in the front and the higher gears in the back)

each click of the shifter stops the cable at exactly the spot it needs to be in to move down the cluster exactly one gear.

Familiarize yourself with your gear shifters. There are two types on most mountain bikes. Above-the-bar, or thumb, shifters and below-the-bar shifters. Thumb shifters consist of one lever that moves toward and away from the rider with the thumb to make the gears shift. Under-the-bar shifters operate via a ratchet system and have two levers, one activated by the thumb to shift to the larger cogs and another by pulling toward the rider with the index finger, releasing the cable to the next smallest cog.

The shifter cables slide inside the cable housing. Your cable housing is lined with materials that allow the free movement of the cable inside the housing. Cable housings fit into cable guides that are brazed onto the frame. Most bikes have slotted cable guides that are very convenient when lubing your housings. A cable that binds inside the housing will cause stiff and inaccurate shifting, especially when moving down the cluster from the larger to the smaller cogs.

MAINTENANCE: Hate to sound like a mountain biking den mother, but keep everything as clean as possible. Keep your cable housings lubed, too, to allow for smooth shifting. Watch for grass and twigs caught in your rear derailleur. Debris in there can clog up the rear cluster, leading to skipping, or it can even break your rear derailleur. Refer to "Dave's 10-Step Program to Keep Your Bike Running in Top Running Condition" (pages 35–38) for details on adjusting your derailleurs.

The freehub protrudes from the rear hub and accepts the rear cassette, or rear cogs. The freehub allows the bike to "freewheel"—to coast without engaging the gears. Inside the freehub body are the palls. Palls are a series of ratchets that operate similarly to a socket wrench. When you push on the pedal the palls engage with the rear hub and move the bike forward. When you're coasting the palls do not engage. This allows the bike to coast without the drive chain being engaged. If this didn't happen when you coasted, the pedals would turn, making standing on your pedals in the downhill impossible. A **freewheel** is an assembly that incorporates the freehub and the rear gear cluster in one unit. Before the introduction of cassette systems, all bikes had freewheels. Freewheels thread onto the rear hub and can be very difficult to remove, since pedaling the bike screws them on tighter and tighter. The freehub and cassette assembly lets you change your rear gears easily.

3. THE FRAME

The frame is the foundation of the bike. It unites all parts and components. The pieces of the frame that we cover are the **top tube, down tube, seat tube, head tube, seat stays,** and **chain stays** (see Figure 2.3).

A few relationships between elements of the frame determine how your bike will ride. For example, the angle between the top tube and the head tube (usually about 72 degrees) dictates how agile the bike is in tight single track. The steeper the angle, the more agile and responsive; the shallower, the more stable and predictable. If you want a bike that will respond instantly in tight single track, then you want a steep head-tube angle; if you want a bike that is stable and smooth on dirt roads, then you want a less steep angle. The other angle that affects bike handling is the seat-tube angle (also usually around 72 degrees). The same general rule applies. The steeper the seat-tube angle, the more agile (and touchy); the shallower the angle, the more secure.

Chain stay length can also have a profound effect on how the bike handles. The shorter the chain stays the more your weight is distributed directly over your rear hub, maximizing rear wheel traction. Longer chain stays give the bike more stability, especially at high speeds, but at the sacrifice of climbing traction.

Frame materials have also undergone many improvements, all with the same goal: to reduce weight while increasing strength and torsional rigidity (see box, page 25). Materials vary from steel alloys to aluminum, carbon fiber, and composite materials. When buying a bike it's important to consider what your needs are in terms of frame materials. Exotic frame materials usually add $200 or more to a comparable bike with a standard chrome-alloy steel frame built in Taiwan. If you're an occasional recreational rider it may not be necessary to pay this premium. If you race, ride often, or are big (190 pounds and up) you may benefit from the added strength and reduced weight of aluminum or composite materials. Carbon fiber frames are not as common in mountain biking because of carbon fiber tubing's brittleness.

MAINTENANCE: Keep an eye on the frame for irregularities like bubbles in the paint or

Fig. 2.3: The frame
a. top tube; b. down tube; c. seat tube; d. head tube;
e. seat stays; f. chain stays
(Photo by Mike Piniewski)

bumps in the tubing. Closely examine the top tube just behind the head tube and the down tube in the same spot. While an irregularity like this may look like just a scratch in the paint job, it could mean something as serious as a crack or bend in the frame. A bent or cracked frame should be replaced immediately. (If your frame breaks, it may make sense to consider purchasing a new bike as opposed to refitting your old components to a new frame.) Many manufacturers will warrant broken frames if you're the bike's original owner and the defect isn't the result of "abuse" (since mountain biking is abusive by nature, such warranties might be difficult to enforce). If you're a big person who rides aggressively, research the warranty before you buy—you'll save headaches in the long run.

STRENGTH VS. WEIGHT

There's a unifying element that connects mountain biking, skiing, surfing, windsurfing, and snowboarding. It's the ratio of strength to weight. In mountain biking, as in other equipment-intensive sports, you want less weight with more strength, to get as much energy to the propulsion of the equipment as possible. When you push on the pedals of your bike, you want as much of your effort as possible to contribute to driving the bike forward. Unfortunately, a lot can happen to dissipate that energy along the way. If you wear sneakers when you ride, the sole flexes and you lose power. If your frame is not stiff, the rear triangle flexes and you lose power. For maximum energy, everything from your shoes to the cranks, chain, frame, and rear hub should be as strong and stiff as possible.

It's possible to manufacture stiff and strong bike components at a very reasonable price. Unfortunately, the bike itself could easily weigh fifty pounds. The general rule of thumb is the lighter a bike gets, the more it costs. The added weight of suspension systems makes shaving weight in other areas even more important. That's one reason we've seen some cool space-age materials in bike construction. For better or worse, this is the future of mountain biking: less weight, more strength, exotic materials, and high prices.

4. THE STEER MECHANISM

The steer mechanism is a simple system that consists of the **headset, fork, stem,** and **handlebars** (see Figure 2.4). The steer tube is the upper part of the fork and slides through the head tube. It's all held in place with the headset. The stem slides into the inside of the steer tube and is secured with a wedge-style binder bolt. The handlebars then slide through the stem and the shifters, grips, and bar ends are attached accordingly.

The most important determination you'll have to make is the amount of rise you want from the stem and the bars. A rise is expressed in degrees; it's the distance the bars or stem rise above the head-tube angle. If you draw a line parallel to the ground, then intersect it with a line drawn at 90 degrees to the length of the head tube—this is the angle that your stem will have with a 0-degree rise. A 10-degree rise is 10 degrees in addition to the angle of the head tube. Generally speaking, the lower the rise the more aggressive the ride. A lower rise puts you down low and over the front of the bike, ideal for climbing, while a larger rise puts your body in a more upright position, better for casual riding and back-road touring.

Handlebars also have a rise of 0 degrees and up. The effect is the same as with the stem. You'll see downhill racers with upswept bars that look almost like they belong on a beach

Fig. 2.4: The steer mechanism
a. headset; b. fork; c. stem; d. handlebars
(Photo by Mike Piniewski)

cruiser. This gives the rider more control and leverage at high speeds. On a general-use bike they'd be useless, but for racing they're very effective.

Headsets. Headsets now come in two types—conventional, which thread onto the steer tube, and the newer sealed style. This newer style of headset is similar to the cartridge bottom bracket in that the bearings are sealed against the weather and the whole thing clamps to an unthreaded steer tube. This means less adjusting and fewer parts to wear out.

MAINTENANCE: Make sure everything is clean and tight and that your headset is not loose. A loose headset will make its signature knocking noise; if it's not fixed, it'll cause enough damage to render the entire headset assembly useless.

5. THE SUSPENSION ASSEMBLY

Before I even attempt to explain how suspension works, I'd like to point something out. Even if you haven't bought your bike yet, you already have an infinitely adjustable, highly efficient suspension system—your arms and legs. When you ride your bike with your butt up off the seat, standing on the pedals, arms flexed and relaxed, you are the suspension system. Next time you ride watch how your arms and legs flex and extend to absorb the impact of the trail. Mechanical suspension systems are meant to complement your organic system; no amount of hardware will replace good riding skills.

Another bit of suspension trivia: fat tires were the first suspension system found on mountain bikes. The bigger the tire, the greater the impact absorption. Tires are adjustable, too; just add air for a stiffer ride. There are limits to the effectiveness of tires as suspension, though. The rigors of mountain bike racing and the desire for more control at higher speeds led to the revolution in mountain bike technology that started in the late 1980s with the introduction of the suspension fork.

Without getting overly technical, I'd like to explain the basic concepts behind mountain bike suspension and why it works. When you hit a rock in the trail with your suspended bike, the fork compresses as it hits to adjust to the change in the surface of the trail. When you pass the rock, the fork returns to its full extension. This results in the rider's upper body following a more or less straight line. On a rigid-frame bike, other than the relatively small amount of absorption that you get from the tire, there is no compression and the wheel has nowhere to go but up. Either the rider lifts the front up over the rock or the front bounces off, driving the handlebars toward the rider or stopping the bike altogether and sending the rider over the handlebars. At high speeds on rough terrain the wheel tends to bounce all over the trail, resulting in a chaotic line of travel and loss of control.

The other benefit of suspension is that as the system responds to changes in terrain, the tires spend more time in contact with the ground than on a rigid-frame bike. This contact is vitally necessary for control. You can't steer or brake a bike when its wheels are in the air. This also results in a less jarring ride, reducing upper body fatigue, ensuring better vision (your eyes aren't bouncing out of your head), and increasing overall rider comfort.

There are downsides to suspension, of course, mainly involving weight and cost. Suspended bikes, especially fully suspended (those with suspension in the front and rear), are heavier and more expensive than rigid-frame bikes. And while the prices of suspended bikes continue to fall, it's often through compromises in areas like frame materials and components.

Fig. 2.5: The front suspension
a. fork crown; b. sliders; c. elastomer/air-oil
cartridge
(Photo by Mike Piniewski)

Front suspension (see Figure 2.5). Most front suspension systems operate with a fork leg slider design and fall into two categories: air-oil and elastomer. Each has two main functions: to absorb impact and to damp oscillations. In air-oil shocks a chamber of air is compressed and offers resistance, cushioning the impact of the trail. In addition, oil in a small reservoir is forced through a valve on the down stroke. After the impact, when the fork extends (rebound), the oil returns to the oil reservoir slowly, controlling the rate of return and further smoothing the ride (damping).

Elastomer forks use urethane bumpers to absorb the shock. Doughnut-shaped pieces of urethane rubber absorb the shock as the fork legs compress. Damping is a function of the rubber's tendency to regain its original shape relatively slowly.

Both systems are adjustable. With air-oil you can adjust air pressure. Heavy riders usually want more pressure, administered through a small needle-valve pump. Higher air pressure means less compression and a stiffer ride. Adjusting elastomer systems requires replacement with rubber of varying densities. Check with the manufacturer of your particular fork for details on how to adjust it.

Both systems can also be adjusted for preload—if you pre-compress the spring, it eliminates the initial phase of compression, giving you a stiffer ride. Elastomer forks usually have an Allen wrench adjustment that compresses the urethane bumpers, while air-oil shocks have dial adjusters that regulate the rate of flow between oil chambers.

Stiction (static friction) results when the fork legs are compressed unevenly. The sliding mechanism binds laterally, which inhibits a smooth rebound phase. Designing shocks with more structural integrity between the fork blades helps with this problem while bikes with one shock in the head tube eliminate stiction altogether.

Rear suspension (see Figure 2.6) operates on the same basic technology as front, but the way it's implemented can vary widely among manufacturers. Most rear-suspended bikes have either an air-oil or an elastomer shock. Suspension is created by isolating the rear triangle from the rest of the frame and attaching at a pivot point. Placement of the pivot point is currently the subject of great debate, and while every manufacturer claims to have the best design, everyone is trying to accomplish the same thing.

Along with added weight, rear suspension has two pitfalls. First, the act of pedaling tends to activate the system, dissipating pedaling energy into the compression of the shock and causing the bike to "pogo" or "biopace" (bounce up and down when the rider is pedaling). This is more of a problem in rear suspension because the rider's weight sits mostly over the rear of the bike and the attachment of the drive train to the rear triangle. Second, putting a hinge in a bike frame lessens torsional stiffness and dissipates additional pedaling energy into frame flex. Depending on where the pivot point is (either low by the chain stays, or high by the seat stays), manufacturers have dealt with the problem of rider-activated suspension in two ways. The system can be "pedal neu-

Fig. 2.6: The rear suspension
a. rear suspension; b. pivot attachments *(Photo by Mike Piniewski)*

tral," meaning it's not activated by pedaling but is still activated by terrain (low pivot point). Otherwise, a manufacturer can cause the system to "lock out" when the rider is pedaling (high pivot point). Unfortunately, the pedal-neutral system can be overly stiff in the descent, and the lockout system does not function when the rider is pedaling—a problem when climbing technical terrain.

Since the low-point design is always active it may be the best for a rider who plans to climb technical trails, since it will help keep both tires on the ground during a climb, while the high-pivot system provides better shock absorption in descents and may be better for downhill racers and those recreational riders who take the lift at ski areas.

Recently some bike manufacturers have used a "unified" rear suspension design. This consists of a one-piece rear triangle that pivots on the down tube forward of the seat tube. Early reports say this is the design of the future because the suspension does not lock out when the rider is pedaling; since the bottom bracket and the chain stays are one structural piece, pogoing and biopacing are largely eliminated.

Confession time: I don't own a fully suspended bike! While I consider front suspension mandatory, rear suspension has too many compromises to make for a good all-around bike. If you want to be a downhill racer, or want to spend all your time riding the lift at Mount Snow, then a fully suspended bike may be for you. But if you want an all-around bike, good in the backcountry, get one with front-only suspension. How many racers have you seen in a cross-country race with fully suspended bikes?

MAINTENANCE: If you have air-oil shocks, make sure to keep enough air in them and that both legs contain equal amounts of air. Uneven air, or uneven damping adjustments, will put uneven stress on the fork legs, causing one leg to take most of the stress from an impact. This could lead to blown seals in one of the fork legs. Have a mechanic experienced in rebuilding forks check for oil leaks and worn seals at least once a season (or more, if you're big and you ride a lot of rough terrain, like me).

Elastomer shocks require virtually no maintenance, although it is possible to crush the bumpers through heavy use.

Since suspension systems have many moving parts it's important to check all mounting bolts (like the fork crown bolts on your front shock) for looseness regularly.

6. THE BRAKE ASSEMBLY

The brakes on a mountain bike are designed to have the maximum braking power possible, in as many different conditions as possible. This is achieved by a number of devices found throughout the braking system.

Nearly all brakes found on mountain bikes today are cantilever brakes. This means that they rotate inward toward the rim on pivot points that are welded to the frame. Over the years, many brake designs were created, seen on bikes for a year or two, and then scrapped. There were power-cam brakes, U brakes, and cantilevers of every shape imaginable. They were mounted on the chain stays and on the seat stays; they were used with motorcycle-style levers and with two-finger levers. Well,

Fig. 2.7: The braking system
a. brake levers; b. cable and
housing; c. brake set;
d. brake pads
(Photo by Mike Piniewski)

eventually the powers that be realized that cantilevers offered the simplest design with the least maintenance and best overall performance.

In simple terms, the brakes are levers with rubber pads, attached to pivots on the frame that are pulled into the rim with cables that are attached to levers mounted on the handlebars. The rider simply squeezes these levers to apply the brakes. This system has been embellished over the years to gain maximum mechanical advantage.

There has been extensive development in the material used in the pads. Since this is *the* interface between the brakes and the wheels, the brake pads are extremely important. Brake pad materials fall into two categories: hard and soft. Softer compounds offer the most braking power with the least amount of noise, but tend to wear rapidly in muddy conditions. (I've been known to go through a brand-new set of pads in one ride!) Hard compounds have a longer life, but can be noisy (anyone who has ridden in the rain and endured the maddening squeal of wet brake pads knows what I'm talking about) and generally don't stop as well as the softer compounds.

Choose your brake pads by analyzing the conditions in your location. If you ride in a mostly dry area, then a soft brake pad material will give you the most braking power. If, on the other hand, you ride in an area with lots of mud, then a harder compound may give you the best wear. Since brake pads can cost as much as $30 a pair, you'll want to get as much life out of them as possible, without compromising performance. It's easy to simply replace the pads on your bike with the same type as was found on it in the showroom. But that doesn't mean there isn't something out there that may work better. Talk to riders in your area. Ask what works for them and what doesn't.

There has been much engineering and design work done on the brake arms to give them as low a profile as possible (to avoid hitting your knee, or something on the trail) while still getting the most leverage (power). In addition, brake levers have evolved to include improved ergonomics; most include cams and return springs for additional mechanical advantage (see Figure 2.7). Cables have been made stiffer to reduce stretching, and new materials have been incorporated into cable housings to reduce friction. The end result is a system that will stop all 200 pounds of me on a dime at a 45-degree angle in the rain and mud. That kind of performance was unheard of as recently as three years ago!

MAINTENANCE: The most important thing to remember in brake maintenance is keeping an eye on the brake pads. Make sure there is plenty of rubber on them. Some brake pad manufacturers have maximum wear lines inscribed on the side of the pad.

As your pads wear and the brake cables stretch it becomes necessary to take up the slack in the cable with the barrel adjusters found on your brake levers. You should be able to squeeze the lever from ½ to 1 inch from the rubber on your handlebars before you have enough braking power to lock the wheels up. If your brakes lock up with the slightest touch of your lever, you need to turn the barrel adjuster so that the pads are not so close to the rim. Brakes adjusted too tightly will lead to over-braking and skidding. If you can squeeze the lever until it touches the grip, you need to turn the barrel adjusters so that the pads are closer to the rim. If your brakes are not adjusted tightly enough, you could find yourself out of control without enough braking power. Remember, your brakes (along with your helmet) are your most important safety tool.

7. THE WHEELS

The wheels of a mountain bike take an incredible amount of abuse. So we've voted them the bike part Most Likely to Be Destroyed Through Heavy Technical Riding. The strength of a wheel comes from the spoke tension. Spokes radiate from the hub attaching to the rim in opposition to each other (see Figure 2.8). This equal tension from both sides is what gives the wheel its structural integrity. Anything that upsets this balance will warp the rim and cause it to wobble as it turns. When a wheel spins perfectly with no wobble, it is said to be "true."

The more spokes in a wheel, the more torsional strength, but also the more weight. Most mountain bikes come with wheels that have thirty-two spokes. Since I weigh 200 pounds I have wheels built for me that have thirty-six

Fig. 2.8: The wheels
a. rim; b. spokes; c. hubs
(Photo by Mike Piniewski)

spokes. I know some even bigger guys who build wheels for themselves with forty spokes—wheels actually meant for tandem bikes. If you're having trouble with wheels constantly getting out of true, consider going to a thirty-six- or forty-hole configuration.

Rim quality can also vary widely. Two ends of a strip of aluminum alloy are joined to form the hoop of a wheel. The two ends are held together with small pins or are spot welded. Generally speaking, rims held together with pins instead of being just welded are stronger. Narrow rims are not necessarily weaker than wider rims, but it can be very difficult to change a tire on a wheel with very narrow rims (17 mm or less).

MAINTENANCE: If you ride in a muddy area the abrasive grit in the mud can wear the side-walls of the rim so thin that they will actually wear through and fail. If you ride often in mud, try to keep your brake pads as clean as possible, especially during long descents, where you'll be on the brakes for extended periods. A rim that's worn out can fail suddenly, and at high speeds can result in a catastrophic crash.

Wheels can also slip out of true very easily. See "Dave's 10-Step Program to Keep Your Bike in Top Running Condition," pages 35–38, for details on how to true your wheel.

TIRES

Tires come in dozens of styles and colors. You can spend anywhere from $15 to $50 on a mountain bike tire, but the conditions in your area and the way you ride should be the deter-mining factors in choosing a tire.

Over the last few years tires have gotten specialized to the point where there are tires designed specifically for front and rear use. Front tires are usually unidirectional—that is, they must be mounted so that the tire tread ro-tates in a specific direction. Most front tires have a chevron design, a series of lugs (the knobby pieces of rubber responsible for trac-tion) arranged in a V pattern, with the narrow part of the V facing the front of the bike. This design tends to push loose material away from the center of the tire, increasing traction and improving the tracking of the front wheel.

Rear tires are designed for maximum trac-tion and come in every lug pattern imaginable. Here in Vermont I look for a rear tire with tall (meaning they stick out from the tire casing as much as 1 inch) lugs that are widely spaced. The tall lugs give excellent traction on wet rock, while the wide spacing prevents the tread pattern from being clogged with mud.

If you live in a relatively dry area this tire wouldn't work very well for you. The tall lugs tend to fold over on hard surfaces, causing in-stability in the rear of the bike when cornering. Instead, choose a tire with more closely spaced lugs with a lower profile to give the bike stabil-ity and predictable tracking.

As with brake pads, tire material varies and falls into two categories: soft and regular com-pounds. Soft compound tires were created to increase traction. They work well in dry condi-tions, but can be slippery on wet rock. Soft tires are also more expensive and wear faster than standard tires, but if you ride on fast, dry hardpack, soft tires can work very well.

Ask your friends and the folks at the bike shop what works best for them. Obviously, your bike will have tires on it when you buy it. Use them for a while before you decide to re-place them. If you're not having any trouble, why replace them before they're worn out?

MAINTENANCE: Make sure that your brake pads are well adjusted and strike the center of the wheel rim. A maladjusted break pad can rub on the tire, ruining the sidewall. Inspect your tires periodically for threadbare side-walls, or any bubbles or irregularities. A tire with thin spots and bubbles will wobble and may incorrectly lead you to think your wheel is out of true.

DAVE'S 10-STEP PROGRAM TO KEEP YOUR BIKE IN TOP RUNNING CONDITION

1. KEEP IT LUBRICATED.

Inadequately lubricated cables are the usual culprit behind stiff or inaccurate shifting. To lube your shifter cables, shift your front and rear derailleurs to their smallest cogs (least amount of cable tension). Remove the cables from the cable guides by slipping the cable through the slot in the guide (most bikes have slotted cable guides; if yours doesn't you'll have to disconnect the cable from the derailleur to get the slack you need). Drip some light-weight oil or spray some Teflon-based lube into both ends of the cable housing and move the housing up and down the length of the exposed cable, working the oil into the cable with your fingers.

To lube brake cables, remove the cable from your brake quick release and the slots in your brake barrel adjusters (if your bike doesn't have slotted barrel adjusters you'll have to disconnect the brake cable at the brake). Spray your shifters, front and rear derailleurs at the pivot points, and jockey pulleys once a month with a lightweight, dry lubricant. And make sure your chain is well lubed with a Teflon-based spray. Avoid using oil on the chain as oil tends to get gunky and collect dirt. A dirty chain will spread abrasive grit through-out the drive train, resulting in excessive wear.

2. KEEP IT CLEAN.

Wash your bike periodically, or after every ride if it gets especially muddy. Rinse your bike with a hose, flush the chain with running water, and make sure the brake pads and rims are free of abrasive grit. A nonaerosol spray glass cleaner works fine on the frame and wheels. After washing, dry your bike with a rag and spray your shifters and derailleurs with a lightweight silicone spray, and your chain with a Teflon-based lube. If you live in a dusty, dry area try blowing the dust off your derailleurs and chain with compressed air in-stead of water. Be sure to wipe off any excess lubricant from your chain so it doesn't be-come a sticky mess.

(continued)

DAVE'S 10-STEP PROGRAM TO KEEP YOUR BIKE IN TOP RUNNING CONDITION (cont'd)

3. REPLACE YOUR PADS.

Don't try to get every last bit of rubber out of your brake pads. Worn pads can damage rims and, in some cases, ride over the rim and shred the sidewall of your tire. When replacing the pads don't forget to toe them in. Set the pad so it lines up with the center of the rim; when the leading edge of the pad is first touching the rim, the rear facing edge is approximately ⅛ inch off the rim. This will prevent the maddening squeal of improperly adjusted brakes.

4. STAY TENSE.

Keep your cable tension properly adjusted. Cables stretch over time. You need to take up the slack in your cables so shifters and brakes function properly. Most shifters and rear derailleurs have barrel adjusters. Adjust them to take up the slack in the cable. With your derailleurs in their smallest cogs, take up any slack by turning the adjuster counterclockwise. You'll know you have the right amount of tension when the derailleur reacts instantly to a shift to the next largest cog and still returns to the smallest cog easily. Brake levers also have barrel adjusters. In the same way you adjusted your derailleur, take up the slack in your brake cables. This will become necessary as your pads wear. Your levers should travel ½ to ¾ inch and should not bottom out on your grip.

5. STAY TRUE.

Spinning true means a wheel doesn't wobble. Knocking about on the trail frequently bangs wheels out of true. Get a spoke wrench that fits your spokes' nipples. Having a truing stand is the best way to get a wheel to spin perfectly, but it can be done using your brake pads as guides. Spin your wheel and watch as the rim passes through the brake pads. If the rim is closer to the pad in one spot than another, your wheel needs truing. Using a felt marker, mark the spot where the rim is closest to the brake pad. Next check all your spokes for looseness; if you have loose spokes, it's likely that they correspond to the area on your rim that is out of true.

DAVE'S 10-STEP PROGRAM TO KEEP YOUR BIKE
IN TOP RUNNING CONDITION (cont'd)

Using the spoke wrench (multisize wrenches are available at most bike shops for about $5), tighten (turn the wrench clockwise as you look at the nipple from above)—half a turn at a time—the spoke(s) on the side *opposite* the spot where the rim is close to the pad. This will pull the rim back away from the pad. Check one side of the rim and then the other. You may also loosen spokes, but start by tightening. When the wheel spins evenly on both sides you've got it. Don't drive yourself crazy seeking perfection. Get it the best you can and be happy!

6. GET YOUR BEARINGS.

Adjusting bearings is about as much fun as doing your taxes. Feel free to skip doing this part yourself and give your friends down at the local bike shop some business. If you do choose to tackle this one you'll need all sorts of weird wrenches and pin-spanners; check at your bike shop to learn which tools you need for your particular bike.

Check for overtight bearings in your hubs by spinning your wheels, by turning your handlebars side to side with the front wheel off the ground (headset), and by back pedaling with your hand (bottom bracket). These points should move smoothly with little or no resistance to motion.

To check the headset for looseness, lock your front brake; grab the handlebars with the front wheel on the ground and rock the front of the bike backward and forward. There should be no knocking or sensation of looseness. To check your wheel bearings, lift the wheel off the ground and try to move it from side to side; once again you should experience no looseness. Check your bottom bracket by leaning over the top tube of your bike, grasping a crank arm (not the pedal) in each hand, and attempting to move the crank arms laterally through their normal range of motion.

To correct a maladjusted bearing assembly, loosen the locking nut. Either loosen or tighten the adjusting nut so the bearing turns freely without looseness. Secure it again by tightening the lock nut.

(continued)

DAVE'S 10-STEP PROGRAM TO KEEP YOUR BIKE IN TOP RUNNING CONDITION (cont'd)

7. KEEP IT TIGHT.

About once a month, tighten all mounting bolts and screws. You want them snug but not to the point where loosening them becomes a pain. Your "tighten up" checklist might include the stem binder bolt, the brake lever or shifter mounting bolts; cable attachments at the brakes and shifters; the seat post or saddle bolt; the quick releases at the wheels (wheel quick releases should be checked and secured every time you ride); water bottle cage mounting bolts, and anything else that is fastened to your bike. This will help prevent your leaving a trail of parts behind you when you rip that ultratechnical section.

8. KNOW WHEN YOU'RE IN OVER YOUR HEAD.

If you have a problem you can't solve on your own, seek professional help! Your bike shop has the tools and expertise to deal with problems you may not even know you have. Say you've installed a new derailleur, but still can't get the damn thing to shift right. Chances are you've bent the derailleur hanger. This is easy to remedy but it involves some expensive and specialized tools. Save yourself some heartache and call a pro!

9. GET AN OVERHAUL.

Once a year, treat yourself (and your bike) to the works. It's an investment in your bike and your sanity. If you live in an area with an off season (is there such a place?) it's best to check in before you store your bike for the winter. Get your bearings regreased, replace your chain, and treat yourself to new brake pads. It'll make life easier when it's time for the first ride of the season, and maintenance in season will be a breeze.

10. PRACTICE, PRACTICE, PRACTICE.

Rehearse important trailside repairs. Remove and replace your rear derailleur, change a tire, put on a patch, take your chain apart. Practice in front of the TV or some other warm cozy spot; that way, your first time won't happen forty miles outside of Podunk when it's going to be dark in half an hour.

3

. . . . .

HOW SLOW CAN YOU GO?

Skills and Techniques
for All Riding Situations

Mental Rehearsal Stimulates Brain
LONDON—*Visualizing a movement, such as a tennis serve or golf swing, turns on 80% of the brain circuits used in the actual movement, brain scans show.*

The mental rehearsal strengthens the brain cell connections needed to smash a winning ace or a booming drive, said Dr. Richard Frackowiak, a professor of cognitive neurology at the Institute of Neurology in London.

The study . . . gives an anatomical explanation for "the common experience of pianists, violinists, tennis players, who very frequently rehearse movements in their minds as a technique for improving performance."

Associated Press, 24 January 1995

By themselves, skill exercises won't help your riding much.

If you don't understand why you're doing a particular exercise, it becomes pointless. To truly benefit from practice, you have to recognize why your bike behaves the way it does, how your bike relates to gravity, how you relate to the bike, and how you both relate to the terrain. You'll be starting with the big picture, not with fragments of it, and finding out not just how, but why. This holistic approach can help first-time riders unlearn what they've been told about riding. Most instructional materials tend to segment the experience, breaking activities down into figures 1, 2, and 3. I believe it's crucial *not* to think in those terms.

I'd like you to unlearn everything you know about bicycles and how to ride them. Wipe the slate clean and open yourself to thinking about you and your bike in a new way. The key is working to integrate all those parts you've seen into a unified, cohesive experience. Understanding something comes with accepting it whole. You need the big picture to comprehend what you're trying to accomplish and why. While we help you understand the purpose behind specific skill exercises, this chapter will try to guide you to that place.

■ ■ ■

Mountain bikes, like their riders, are slaves to the laws of physics. By thinking about four principles that govern practically the entire mountain biking experience, you can gain a better understanding of the elements of mountain biking—the essential ingredients that control every ride. Thinking about them while you ride will enrich your riding skills as much as any exercise will. Through them, you'll gain a solid base to comprehend those exercises in the first place.

1. Inertia. The principle of inertia holds that moving bikes tend to stay in motion and still bikes don't move. That's why you can "fake" your way through technical terrain by maintaining momentum—your bike wants to keep moving.

Hesitation—and the momentum meltdown that follows—is often to blame for dabbing. This is true whether you're riding uphill, downhill, or cornering. Think of your ride as a smooth, continuous line unbroken by starts, stops, or changes in speed. Anticipate the next section before you're in it, visualize the line you want to take, and then see yourself doing it. Maintaining momentum will get you through most riding situations. It takes a leap of faith to charge through intimidating terrain, and with the correct body position you can learn how to "ride it out."

Sometimes terrain will not allow you to fake your way through. There may be a huge rock smack-dab in the middle of the trail, or a log down at an impossible angle. This is when slower is better. On the other hand, don't try recklessly zooming through a trail; you must be able to tell the difference between what is rideable and what isn't. Discovering the difference takes time, and what is rideable for one person may forever be unrideable to you. Learn your limits and expand them carefully.

2. Gyroscopic action. As long as the wheels keep turning, the bike wants to stay upright. When you're "faking" your way through a technical section, the gyroscopic action of the wheels helps to keep you upright and inertia keeps you moving forward.

You can see the gyroscopic effect yourself by taking your bike's front wheel out of the fork, grabbing the hub from both sides, and spinning the wheel as hard as you can. Try to turn the wheel on its side; if it spins fast enough, you'll feel the force trying to keep it upright. If not for this principle, bikes would just tip over. It all depends on how fast your wheels are turning, which is why forward momentum is so important.

At slow speeds, the gyroscopic action of the wheels diminishes—and a completely different set of riding skills becomes important. We've all felt how a slow-moving bike wants to tip over. Your balance and ability to hold your bike in line come into play here. You need to be able to balance the bike without the benefit of the gyroscopic action of the wheels. Say, for instance, you're riding down the trail and see a huge rock in your path. Charging over it will result in a major endo and face plant. The only way around it is a narrow, circuitous path that changes direction ten times in twenty feet. You could get off and walk, but part of riding is learning to negotiate the obstacle at a very slow speed.

Learn to balance your bike and stay upright while the bike is nearly motionless (this is called "a trackstand"; we'll cover it later in this chapter). The ability to hover on the trail gives you the time needed to pick your line. Try riding your favorite technical trail as slow as possible. You'll gain the balance you need to negotiate tight, technical terrain.

3. Traction. *Strive to achieve equal downward force on each tire.* You have the most control over your bike when both wheels are in solid contact with the dirt; a suspension bike works because the suspension keeps both wheels on the ground, increasing traction and control. You're striving for a sort of equilibrium, a homeostasis, a balance between the front and rear.

When you're riding uphill, gravity weights the rear of the bike. Your front wheel tends to lift off the trail as a result, wandering in a climb and making it difficult to hold your line. For this reason, riders keep their bodies low and forward when climbing. On downhills, body weight tilts to the front wheel, so we keep our weight to the back of the bike to compensate for the effects of gravity. The goal of these shifts is the same; a *net equal balance* on both tires. The level at which you compensate varies every second with changing terrain. It's necessary to make thousands of adjustments in your body position on the bike in order to allow your bike to follow the path you've chosen.

4. Entropy. This is the tendency of the universe toward chaos—to move from order to disorder. When you drop a glass on the floor it shatters and scatters across the room. When your tires bounce, slide, and skid on a technical trail, your bike's path becomes chaotic. The chaos is magnified by every stick and rock— order to disorder.

To fight the effects of entropy, your body makes thousands of tiny corrections. Sometimes it's as subtle and unconscious as a tiny shift in weight to one side. Sometimes it's as dramatic as popping a wheelie to cross a ditch. We've all heard of "muscle memory," how the body learns to work on autopilot by performing an action over and over. When you walk, you don't consciously think about placing your left foot in front of your right and moving forward. Same with mountain biking; the more you do it, the more automatic it becomes. By spending time on technical trails, you'll feel elements of riding become second nature. You'll be able to tackle terrain that once scared you—except now you'll be thinking about what to have for supper.

In a funny way your body becomes motionless. If someone could only see your upper body on a trail, it wouldn't appear to be moving. In skiing, it's called a "quiet upper body"; the skier's upper body would appear smooth if you masked her or his legs. This state of being represents your body's ability to compensate for entropy; it is order imposed on a chaotic situation.

It's up to you and your body to compensate for (and take advantage of) the effects of inertia, gyroscopic action, traction, and entropy. We all operate under these same principles every moment of every day, whether we're walking, driving, playing basketball, or riding our mountain bikes. You can learn to control them as much as they control you.

■ ■ ■

Good things come in fours. Now that we've covered the four principles that govern every ride, it's time to explore the four actions that come into play in every riding situation, regardless of terrain:

1. Legs push cranks, cranks move chain, chain drives wheel. *Result:* Bike moves forward.
2. Hand pushes lever, lever pulls cable, cable activates derailleur, derailleur moves chain through the gears. *Result:* Gear ratio changes to allow pedaling efficiency in varying terrain.
3. Fingers grip lever, lever pulls cable, cable pulls brake mechanism, brake mechanism pushes brake pad onto rim. *Result:* Bike slows or stops.
4. Rider varies body weight distribution on the bike. *Result:* Bike and rider compensate for varying terrain.

Your challenge, of course, is to combine these actions into skills that enhance your riding. There are thousands, if not millions, of different combinations. Squeeze your front brake, get up off the seat, power up a short incline, and so forth. Becoming adept at these skills will equip you to ride anything.

BASIC SKILLS

Getting your first mountain bike is like getting a new roommate at school. At first things are a little awkward. You're not quite sure what kind of reaction you'll get when you have to put your foot down. But in the end you realize you've made a lifelong friend.

Get to know your bike before you take on big challenges. Ride around the neighborhood. Ride to work. Get a rack or wear a backpack to carry your stuff. Use your bike as transportation. It'll make being on your bike seem natural, something you do every day. And as a bonus you'll be a more fit, more earthfriendly, happier human being.

Try to use all the parts of your bike. Shift up and down the gear clusters front and back. Test your brakes, understand how they work and what they can do. The limiting factor in mountain biking is the rider, not the bike. Trust your bike, believe in it and what it can do, but also respect it and know its limitations. With persistence, preparation, and the right attitude, you and your bike can do things you've never dreamed possible.

Shifting and Cadence

Cadence is the speed at which your legs turn the cranks. The ideal in biking, whether it be road or mountain, is to reach a steady, even cadence in every riding situation. In a perfect mountain biking world your legs would spin at 70 to 90 rpm, whether uphill, on a flat surface, or through mud. Spinning 70 to 90 rpm gives you the most efficient use of your legs and is the most sustainable pace over time. Pushing along at 40 rpm in too big a gear is stressful to the knees, and also will result in premature fatigue of the quadriceps muscles of your legs.

When it comes to mountain biking, spin is in. Think of your legs as spinning in smooth, complete circles, not pushing one pedal down and then the other. Unify the motions. Pull up on your pedals with one foot at the same time as the other foot begins its down stroke. Learn by feel when you're in the right gear. Use a high enough gear to power the bike forward, but not so high that you are bearing down unnecessarily.

Use the second hand on your wristwatch to determine your cadence. Count once for each time your right foot is at the bottom of its pedal stroke. Count for fifteen seconds and multiply by four. This number is the revolutions per minute that the pedals are spinning. Get to know what the proper cadence feels like.

To maintain a 70 to 90 rpm cadence in varying terrain, you need to be able to shift quickly, confidently, and appropriately. This skill takes a while to develop, and even the best riders mis-shift from time to time, but with time shifting becomes second nature. Remember, you can only shift *while pedaling*. The system doesn't function when the bike is at rest.

A few more tips to help you become shiftier:

1. Shift early. Even with recent improvements in shifting mechanisms, the more of a load there is on the chain, the more reluctant your bike will be to shift. This is especially true of gear changes in the front chain rings and in shifts to smaller cogs in the rear. (Hyperglide cogs are designed to assist shifts going up the cluster from smaller to larger cogs.) Instead of fighting the gearing, shift just before you're about to hit a new section of trail. If you're approaching a hill, shift just as your front wheel starts up the hill. If you're still a little tentative, shift into a lower gear well back from the start of the hill and enter the climb slowly in the proper gear to get to the top at a pace you can maintain.

If you find yourself in too big a gear halfway up the hill, I know a trick that will allow you to downshift smoothly. Try to sprint for a short distance up the hill. Gain some momentum and then back off. Using the momentum you've established, spin your pedals with the least amount of pressure possible on your chain. At the same time shift your gears. This will take the heavy load off your chain and allow you to shift gears smoothly without that annoying clanking and grinding of a loaded chain.

It's a little easier to make a gear change riding downhill, but you still want to get into the proper gear early in your descent. On a rough downhill, it's important to take up as much slack in the chain as possible. Even if you don't complete one pedal stroke during your descent, putting your chain in the large chain ring up front lets you take up much of the slack in your chain. It can also minimize chain slap, the nerve-wracking pounding a loose chain makes on top of your drive-side chain stay.

2. Shift often. For top pedaling efficiency, shift as often as necessary to maintain that 70 to 90 rpm pace. It shouldn't take an undue effort to maintain this pace. If you feel you're overexerting, shift to a lower gear but keep your cadence the same. If you feel like you're spinning but not going anywhere, shift to a bigger gear.

3. Forget what I said. Having told you about the ideal cadence I feel obliged to mention situations when you won't be able to achieve this ideal. In steep climbs, for example, you may have to hold your cadence to 40 rpm to keep from burning out before you reach the top. Highly technical terrain also requires slow rpm because you need to maneuver through tight sections. Do what works best for you in special situations.

UPHILL

It's your first ride of the season. You round a corner and there it looms: the big climb, the wall, Mount Everest. You wonder how the hill could have become steeper since last October. You doubt you can make it to the top. You consider turning around, buying some Ho-Hos, and snuggling up to watch *The Price Is Right*.

Stop! It's time for a major attitude adjustment. Don't hate hills. Hills make you stronger. You just need to learn how to like them, love them, seek them out. The longer the hill the better. Steeper equals more fun. And always remember: for every uphill, there has to be a downhill.

There are some basic rules you can follow to make those hill climbs less painful:

1. Stay in your seat. Standing while pedaling uphill takes weight off the rear wheel—and results in loss of traction and spin-outs, especially in loose or muddy conditions. This doesn't mean that you can just sit there; you still need to move on your bike. Slide forward on your seat as the terrain gets steeper. Push your handlebars out in front of you to handle an abrupt change in elevation. You still need to be dynamic. Sitting while climbing requires much less energy than standing. You'll be able to last much longer by staying seated.

2. Get your weight over the front wheel. While it's important to keep the rear wheel weighted for traction, it's also important to keep the front tire firmly in contact with the trail. When you climb, your mountain bike's front end tends to become lighter. This can produce a loss of traction and steering control, causing the front tire to wander. It becomes difficult to hold your line and pick your way through obstacles in the trail. Weight the front wheel to maintain traction and steering control.

You can accomplish this by using your upper body to hold down the front end of the bike. While staying firmly planted in your seat, lower your torso forward. Slide up slightly on your seat to accentuate the body-forward position. Keep a loose hold on the grips, arms bent and tucked in; avoid pulling up on the handlebars. Generally, your back should be at a 30-degree angle to the top tube, or even less of an angle—almost parallel—in the steepest terrain. How low and forward you are will depend on how steep the terrain is. Constantly adjust your body position to the changing terrain.

3. Slow down! Attacking a hill like a lunatic zooms you to maximum oxygen uptake very quickly. Halfway up you'll run out of steam, feel like you're going to toss your cookies, and ultimately hate all hills everywhere. Instead of going as fast as you can up the hill, try going as slow as possible, one pedal stroke at a time. This will give you a base line to build upon. After a couple of weeks of slow hill climbs, pick up the pace. See how it feels. If it's too much, pull back a little. Learn to read a hill and know what kind of pace you can maintain to the top.

4. Relax! You've probably got a hold on the grips that'll leave permanent fingerprints in the rubber. Concentrate on relaxing your up-

per body. A tight grip produces excessive muscle tension, premature fatigue, a sore neck and lower back muscles, and an unhappy mountain biker. Keep your thumbs and fingers on top of the bars to avoid what we call "the white-knuckled grip of death." Simply rest your

Use your upper body to weight the front wheel when climbing.

hands on the bars, using them to guide your bike as you climb. Your bike is your friend, not a wrestling opponent. Avoid flaring your arms out to the side. Besides looking silly, that position tends to shift the weight of your upper body to your hands and forearms, and again causes muscle fatigue.

5. Pick your line. Sound familiar? Uphill, the line you pick will depend on the abruptness of elevation changes and trail surface condi-

When the going gets steep, the rider gets forward.

tions. The more gradual the changes in elevation, the easier it will be to clear a section. Of course, if the gradual line is covered with mud and has running water—but you spot a steeper, drier line—you may want to reconsider. Or if the low part of the trail is loose and dry, you may want to pick a higher, steeper line that is hardpacked. One thing you shouldn't do, though, is ride off the trail; this could lead to erosion and trail damage. Eventually, you'll feel comfortable using common sense and experience to make those decisions.

6. Use your upper body to move the bike forward. In technical terrain, you often encounter abrupt elevation changes. Picture a shelflike rock, rising about 24 inches, in the middle of the trail. Riding it is the only way to continue without dabbing. You hop the front wheel up onto it, and when your rear wheel reaches the rock you bear down on the pedals to try to get on top of the rock, but you spin out and stall. What could you have done differently?

Try using upper-body strength to move the bike past the obstacle. When the front wheel reaches the top of the rock, draw the handlebars toward your chest and then explode your arms outward, pushing the bike out in front of you. At the same time, stand and hop the bike on top of the rock without pedaling. Practice a few times going up a curb. You'll find this skill very helpful when traction is questionable.

7. Ignore your friends. When you ride with others, it's rare to find someone whose abilities perfectly match yours. There's nothing more dangerous to your happiness and well-being than trying to keep up with someone faster than you. Sure, it's good to ride with someone who'll push you, make you reach a little bit more. But too much is poison—it creeps into your being and makes you hate your best friend. You could stop riding with him or her, or forget your ego and go at your own pace. You aren't a bad person because you can't keep up; what have you got to prove? Agree ahead of time that whoever's out in front (it could be you, couldn't it?) will wait at predetermined spots. That way no one will be anxious about getting left behind.

STARTING WHEN YOU'RE ALREADY ON A HILL

If you stall during a climb, try not to walk your bike. I have an unwritten rule: if I stall in a climb I have to start the ride again where I stopped, no walking. It may mean hanging around for a few minutes and catching your breath, but in the long run it will improve your riding skills.

Find a small level spot or rock to rest your rear tire. Shift your bike to its lowest gear. Position your cranks so one is at the beginning of its down stroke. Stand over your bicycle with one foot on the raised pedal. Start off gently with the first down stroke, to allow the other foot to be placed on the pedal. Then, with a burst of pedaling, get your weight forward and establish your momentum. At first your cranks should be turning at about 80 rpm. Once you've established your momentum, back off to a comfortable pace and head on up the hill. This is what meeting challenges is all about. It may be easier to walk, and getting on and off the bike may be frustrating, but the psychic rewards at the top of the hill will be worth it.

A couple of years ago I was gazing out the window of my office at Mount Snow, looking at the last section of the downhill course as it approaches the base area. The course zigzags down the grassy ski slope, a thin dirt stripe making about eight sharp switchback turns. Suddenly an idea popped into my head. Why don't I ride *up* the downhill course?

Of course, it was 12 noon, about 90 degrees in the bright sunshine, but then I never said I had any common sense. One thing became obvious as I grunted and gasped up the hill: going as slowly as possible was the only way to the top without dabbing. I held back in the less steep sections, leaving energy to power up the steeper, looser sections.

Struggling to keep my heart rate below 200, I also had to negotiate sharp, sudden turns. As I came into the turns, I slid forward so that I was perched on the very end of the saddle. Keeping my weight forward and low, I slowed almost to a stop to set myself up for the turn. Then, with an explosion (well, a small burst anyway) of pedaling energy I pointed my front wheel exactly where I wanted my bike to go and sprinted until I cleared the steepest part of the turn and then restarted the how-slow-can-you-go routine. I did make it to the top, and the experience confirmed some basic principles of climbing as taught at the Mountain Bike School.

The moral: learn to judge a hill by steepness and length, look ahead, and pace yourself accordingly. When approaching a steep pitch, shift early. While shifting mechanisms have come a long way in the last few years, derailleurs don't like to shift with a heavy load on the chain. This is particularly true of the front derailleur. Maintain your momentum during the climb, pick a pace you can maintain to the top, but hold back a bit, leaving room for powering through rough areas like loose rocks or a downed tree.

DOWNHILL

I think of technical downhill riding as the essence of mountain biking. If you can ride a bike successfully down a narrow, loose, rock-strewn trail, then anything else will seem easy by comparison. The basics:

1. Stand on your pedals, weight back, butt up off the seat. Keep your knees bent, and let your legs flex to absorb the shock of the terrain. Push your handlebars out in front of you. Compensate for the effects of gravity by weighting the rear wheel.

Keeping your weight back isn't static. You have to constantly adjust. If you're turning a

Create a platform with your pedals for stability in descending.

The steeper the terrain, the farther back you go.

corner, you need to keep your body perpendicular to the ground while pushing the bike into the turn. On very steep terrain and drop-offs, you might have your butt so far back that the seat or even the rear tire will be in front of you. If you suddenly reach a short, flat section or an uphill, your weight must shift forward, over the front wheel.

The ability to be mobile on your bike, to shift your weight quickly and confidently, allows you to compensate for the effects of gravity and make these transitions. And the ability to create a stable platform brings it all together. You build a stable platform by rising off the seat, balancing on the pedals, and actually standing. Stand on your pedals with the crank arms in a horizontal position, parallel to the ground. Extend your legs, keeping your butt off the seat and slightly back. Relax and flex your arms slightly. Standing gives you the stability you need to adjust your body position in response to changing terrain. Try flexing and extending your legs, moving from side to side. Feel how a changing, dynamic stance affects your bike handling.

The purest application for building a platform comes in downhills. You absolutely have to stand on the pedals to stay stable. Simply because of gravity, there's more weight on the front tire going downhill. So you want to emphasize the rear of the bike to compensate. Shifting your weight to the back of the bike distributes the weight where it belongs—to both tires, not just one. Emphasize weight on your rear wheel. Keep the front wheel light, so if it comes across an obstacle it'll "float" over it instead of digging in.

To get first-timers at the Mountain Biking School comfortable with standing on the pedals, we actually take the seats off their bikes. That helps wean them from depending on the seat. For road-bike veterans, the seat becomes something to unlearn once you start to mountain bike. You can't sit and pedal over rough terrain the way you would on a paved road. Here, the seat's a crutch and you can't use it (unless, of course, you're going uphill). Take away the crutch, and you'll learn to live without it.

If you have a real phobia about standing on the pedals, find someone strong to hold your handlebars in place and straddle your front wheel for support while you build a platform. Then try shifting your body position as your helper steadies the bike. Your ultimate goal is freedom of movement, in any direction, while on the platform. Once you feel more relaxed, start practicing it in a place where you're totally comfortable—your yard, a parking lot, wherever. That'll help you gain confidence and not obsess on the terrain.

2. Pick your line. Anticipate terrain before your bike is there. Vary your focus from just in front of your wheel to as far down the trail as you can see and back again. That way, you can maneuver through the close range obstacles while keeping an eye on what's approaching.

3. Use your front brake. A lot of my students seem to think they shouldn't use the front brake in descents. It's a myth. Up to 90 percent of your braking power comes from the front brake. Used improperly it will send you over the handlebars, but you *need* that power to stop quickly and reliably.

To brake in a downhill, apply your rear brake first. Don't forget that your weight should be back over the rear wheel. Then *gradually* apply your front brake until you've got the braking power you need. Practice on smooth terrain and see how quickly you can stop when both brakes are applied aggressively.

With both wheels sharing the brake load, you can stop quickly without locking up your rear wheel and skidding. Although locking up your rear wheel and skidding through a turn can be effective (downhill racers use this technique all the time), it's highly eco-unfriendly

and a major factor in trail erosion. Instead of skidding through a turn, control your speed above the turn and accelerate through it.

Check that your brake levers are properly adjusted. You should not be able to bottom out the lever on your grips, but you need enough lever travel to have varying degrees of braking power. Too-tight levers will cause premature lockup and skidding; loose levers will bottom out on the grip, cutting down braking power and increasing your chances of losing control. The right amount of lever travel also depends on the size of your hands. Since women generally have smaller hands than men, they need levers with less travel. Many levers have adjustable reach; your local bike shop can help adjust yours.

4. Brake before you reach rough terrain. There's more stability in acceleration than in deceleration. When approaching a technical section of trail, control your speed before you reach the difficult part. Braking in loose gravel, rocks, or logs creates instability and loss of control. Instead, check your speed before approaching a difficult section. You may even want to come nearly to a complete stop so that you can pick your line. Then ease off your brakes and accelerate through the section. Remember, stay off the seat, keep back, and make your front wheel as light as possible. In a long section, you may have to hit the brakes periodically to control your speed, but try to find an area that's relatively smooth, slow down, and then start another acceleration phase.

5. Manage your fear. Over the years, I've uncovered what's at the root of difficulty in technical downhill trails: *fear,* either too much or not enough. Too much fear results in systemic hesitancy, a failure to trust the situation and your bike. Sure, you could fall, but if you're not out of control and going Mach 10, what are you afraid of? You might get a bruise, your friends may laugh at you, but you need to set these concerns aside and be willing to take risks. It's the only way you'll progress. Don't hurt yourself. But *do* stretch, push limitations, reach for a goal. Pick away at your fear, let it erode each time you ride.

The opposite, of course, is *not enough* fear. This is usually the realm of fifteen- to twenty-five-year-old males, a group I call the Testosterone Club. A fear deficit usually results in too much speed and not enough common sense. Too much too soon results in the terrain getting away from you. Instead of reacting to the terrain, you just hang on until the next crash. It's much easier to teach a hesitant rider to reach a bit than it is to rip the headphones off a seventeen-year-old and make him respect the terrain. Unfortunately, it's often a major crash with injuries—their own or friends'—that wakes them up.

The middle ground is a level of fear appropriate for the situation. If you're twenty miles from help looking down at a monster downhill strewn with rocks you *should* be scared. I'm not telling you to avoid riding it (though that might be a very good decision), but the appropriate level of fear instills respect for the terrain.

CORNERING

Most mountain bike tires have been designed with special lateral lugs (knobs) to provide secure cornering and predictable tracking. To get the most out of this design, it's important to lean your bike in a turn and distribute your body weight over these lateral lugs.

1. Steer by leaning the bike. As with skis, you need to set a bike's tire on its edge to make it turn. The faster you travel, the more this is true. If you tried to steer a bike traveling at high speeds (10 mph or more) by turning the handlebars, the front end would jackknife and you'd take a nasty spill. Instead, push your handlebars into the turn. While moving the bars lateral to the bike and down toward the ground, move your body in the opposite direction. This will keep your body upright in relation to the ground and will distribute your weight directly above the corresponding tire lugs. Position the cranks so that the pedal on the inside of the turn is at the top of its pedal stroke. This gives you a counterpoint to push on and prevents you from hitting obstacles that may be in the trail. In high-speed cornering, removing your foot from the inside pedal and extending your leg out from the bike, outrigger style, can greatly improve stability in the turn.

2. Brake before the turn. As you read in the section on downhill skills, there's more stability in acceleration than deceleration. Control your speed above the turn and accelerate out of it. I've seen many a downhill racer reach Mach speed on the straightaways, only to hit the turn too fast. Braking in the corner causes loss of momentum and, as in the case of the downhill racer, actually reduces your overall time.

3. Make smooth transitions. Practice transitioning from one turn to the next on your slalom course or on a snaky single track. Lean the bike into the turn, then bring it back up. Tip your bike in the opposite direction. Feel how your body moves from one side of the bike to the other. Make these transitions as smooth and seamless as possible.

ADVANCED SKILLS

Log Jumping

You're riding down the trail. A log appears before you. About 10 inches in diameter, it looms, daring you to jump it. You can either get off your bike and ignore the challenge of this dead piece of wood, or laugh in its mossy face and ride right over it.

1. Maintain your momentum. You need to maintain your forward momentum to clear the log without tipping over. If you have enough forward momentum you should be able to clear the log without using pedal power. If the log is uphill from your approach you'll need to pedal hard to establish your momentum. If the approach is downhill, merely letting off the brakes may be enough. Either way, the right amount of momentum is determined by your experience and skill level. Falls are common when learning to jump a log, so start slow and discover in increments the right amount of momentum for a given situation.

2. Approach the log at as close to a 90-degree angle as possible. If the log is lying in the trail at an odd angle, swing wide and approach it on a line as close to perpendicular as possible. Jumping a log at a shallow angle

Put your weight over the inside edge of your tire in
the turn.

tends to deflect the front wheel along the length of the log, sliding it across—and dumping you aside.

3. Stand on the pedals and unweight the front wheel. Timing at this phase of the operation is key. When you stand on your pedals, with your weight back, give the handlebars a tug up and back. Time it as if you were to lift the front wheel off the ground and set it down again, either on top of the log or on the far side. With smaller logs (up to 6 inches in diameter), it's not necessary to actually lift the front wheel off the ground. Merely getting back and tugging slightly will lighten the front end sufficiently to allow it to roll over the log. With larger logs, you'll need to actually lift the wheel and place it on top of the log. This takes both more effort and more momentum. For larger logs, it can be helpful to add a pedal stroke at the same moment that you lift on the handlebars. With the bike in a large enough gear, the force of a pedal stroke tends to lift the front, making it easier to pop up that front end.

Students new to log jumping often jump the gun and lift their bars too soon. The result: front wheel comes up, falls, hits the log head-on, rider flies over handlebars. Again, if the rider doesn't unweight the front wheel soon enough, it'll hit the log head-on with the same result.

4. Move your weight forward to unweight the rear wheel. Once you've cleared the log with your front tire, shift your weight forward to lighten the rear end and allow it to roll over the log. As the front end drops onto the trail, shift your weight, once again, toward the back. If you feel momentum dissipating, throw in a pedal stroke when you feel the rear tire is on top of the log.

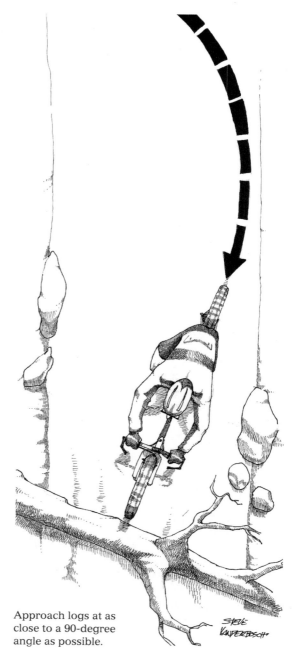

Approach logs at as close to a 90-degree angle as possible.

Compress your tires in preparation for bunny hopping.

Remember to visualize log jumping as a complete, fluid movement with no beginning and no end. Practice jumping small objects and work your way up. Put a broomstick in your driveway. Lift your front wheel as you approach it and set it down again on the other side. Try to land squarely on top. By practicing in this way you'll develop an ability to aim for objects with your front tire, and build skill and confidence as well.

BUNNY HOPPING

Bunny hopping is the ability to jump the bike with both wheels coming off the ground simultaneously. To me, bunny hopping has always been the most difficult skill to teach. It takes superior timing, good reflexes, a strong upper body, and an instinctive sense of where your bike's center of gravity is located.

Several years ago I was riding my bike on New York's Upper West Side. As I motored across Broadway, trying to keep up with car traffic, I saw a *huge* dead rat lying directly in my path. This rat was so big (how big was it?) that for a second I thought it was a dead dog. I was going too fast to avoid it. There were several dozen pedestrians in the intersection waiting to cross. I had no choice. I crouched down on my bike and with an explosive burst I sprang up, lifting the bike up and over the rotting rodent flesh. As I sped through the intersection I could hear the crowd of pedestrians cheer my Olympic-class feat. This was certainly one of my finest moments, and nicely illustrates the value of being able to bunny hop.

Think of your body as a spring coil. When you're standing normally the spring is relaxed. Crouch on the balls of your feet with your knees bent. Now the spring is loaded. By pushing off the balls of your feet and explosively extending your legs, you release the energy stored in the loaded spring. This is the basic principle in bunny hopping. By crouching over your bike and rapidly moving your body upward it's possible to lift both wheels of the bike at the same time.

1. Stand on your pedals and bounce the bike up and down. Execute a trackstand as outlined in the single track section later in this chapter. Pick a soft grassy spot so you don't get too beat up when you tip over. As you hover and move slowly, flex and extend your knees without trying to jump the bike. Keep your upper body parallel to the top tube of the bike, shoulders over the handlebars, and crouch low so that your crotch is about 2 inches from the top tube at the bottom of the compression. As you sink toward the ground, push down on the handlebars. Feel how the tires compress as you push down. Both tires should compress equally. Try to compress the tires as much as possible, and then move your body upward. Think of it as one movement, up and down. Follow through with your entire body as the bike begins to lift. Don't pull up on the handlebars; instead, keep your elbows locked and bring the front of the bike upward with you as you lift. Continue to bounce up and down, finding the fore-and-aft body position, the "sweet spot," that causes the wheels to sink and rise equally.

2. Get it up! Once you've found the sweet spot, exaggerate your movements. Drop down low and spring up, pulling from the center of the bike, not the handlebars. It's not feet on pedals or hands on bars that make the bike rise, it's your entire body. You'll probably feel one wheel come off the ground more than another; keep experimenting with your body position until you find the sweet spot. Keep practicing. You'll feel how more compression brings more height in the jump. Get completely comfortable with stationary jumping before moving on to the next step.

3. Move it! Once you're able to get both wheels off the ground reliably you can add some linear movement to the mix. Go back to the broomstick in your driveway. With moderate forward momentum (you'll need more momentum with a bunny hop than with an ordinary log jump), jump the bike over the stick, trying not to hit it at all. Practice on small objects, since an ill-timed bunny hop over a large object can wreck both your bike and your body. Practice your timing so you can predict where your bike will land. Gradually increase the diameter of the object until you feel comfortable trying it out on the trail.

WHEELIES

We've all seen these guys who can wheelie all the way from New York to Vermont. Showoffs! What good is a wheelie anyway? Actually, it *is* great for crossing a ditch or jumping a curb. By setting your front wheel down on the far side of a ditch or on top of a curb you can avoid many an endo. Because your front wheel is in the air you can't auger into the ditch and fly over the handlebars.

Remember what I said about a downward

Pop a wheelie to keep your front wheel out of a ditch.

pedal stroke lifting the front of the bike when jumping a log? Every action has an opposite and equal reaction. In addition to moving the chain and driving the bike, a downward pedal stroke also tends to lift the front of the bike. By accentuating this effect and maintaining a balance you can keep the front of your bike off the ground while continuing to move forward.

1. Lean back. Stay in your seat and tug on the handlebars, then throw your shoulders back. Be careful not to lean too far, though; you might go over backward and land on your butt with the bike on top.

2. Keep pedaling. It's the combination of weight distribution and the levering action of pedaling that keeps the front end up. If the cranks stop turning, the front of the bike will drop.

3. Pick the right gear. Get into a gear big enough to keep the front wheel up in the air. Too small a gear simply does not exert enough force to do this.

4. Practice. Don't start by trying to get your front wheel 3 feet off the ground. Instead, pull on the handlebars as if you were going to jump a log; instead of going up and immediately down, try to keep the front of the bike up as long as you can. You'll be able to increase the height and duration of your wheelie gradually as your confidence grows.

TERRAIN ISSUES

SINGLE TRACK

Imagine recording types of biking terrain on slips of paper. Write *uphill* on fifty slips, *downhill* on thirty-seven, add nine *log jumps*. Don't forget *rocks* (twenty-four) and *slippery roots* (thirteen). Now put the papers in a big paper bag and shake vigorously. Dump on a table and arrange in the order in which they came out of the bag.

This is what you get when you ride single track—a shoulder-width, rapid-fire barrage of every mountain biking obstacle you can imagine. Single track is where you put together everything you've learned (or haven't learned) about mountain biking—it's the testing ground, the real world. So how do you ride single track? What is the unifying theme of single track? **Reaction time**—the time it takes for you to react appropriately to incoming information. It's a function of the nervous system, and like your muscles and cardiovascular system, the nervous system needs exercise to perform at its peak, so you can react quickly. Here are a few exercises you can do to develop your reaction time:

1. Trackstands. To perform a trackstand is to be able to stand still on your bike without touching a foot to the ground. Practice them to build your ability to hover for a few seconds before you pick your line in front of an obstacle. Lock both brakes; while standing on your pedals, slightly forward of your seat, maintain forward pedal pressure. Your shoulders should be directly above the handlebars. As you start to tip to one side, turn your front wheel away from the direction you're tipping. Move your upper body with the handlebars, keeping your shoulders perpendicular to the front wheel. Less is more with trackstands—subtle movements will keep you from lurching side to side. If you overcorrect, you'll tip in the other direction. Follow the same procedure to stay upright. If you feel that you're going to go over, release your brakes, move forward a couple of pedal strokes, and try again. As you improve, the movements required will become more and more subtle. The smallest movement will keep you upright. Practice trackstands on a soft surface like grass so you won't hurt yourself if you fall. Stick with it, and soon you'll be able to "float" with the best of them.

2. Slow riding improves your balance, which becomes critical on the trail. Find a technical trail, preferably one you know well. Ride as slowly as you can. Play with the line you pick—instead of the easiest or most direct, choose the most difficult, circuitous route. Come to a full stop, hover, then release your brakes and start pedaling. By applying both brakes and pedaling against them you'll gain the stability needed to go extra slow. You'll also teach yourself how to ride without momentum and the gyroscopic effect of the wheels, relying on your own balance and reaction-time skills instead.

3. Set up a slalom course on an open hillside. By running gates you can improve your ability to make sudden turns and react to changing terrain. Use flimsy sticks that will break if you hit them or anything soft (empty milk jugs work well) to make your gates. Make a row of at least ten gates over 100 feet. Try different configurations; make some turns very tight and others wide and sweeping. Practice coming in close to the gates. Lean into the turns, then make your transition into the next turn as graceful and smooth as possible. As you get more comfortable and familiar with the course you've set, work on increasing your speed. This exercise will improve your stability in the turns and will help you get the feel for tire traction and turning control.

SOFT SURFACES

Momentum, once again, is the key to clearing soft trail conditions. If you see a patch of mud, sand, or snow, look ahead and try to determine the best way through. Look for the line where the loose material is most shallow, or where firmer terrain pokes through the goop. In this case it's best not to hover and look for your line because you will not be able to regain your momentum when you hit the bog.

Once you've picked your line (if you haven't, keep moving anyway—you might get lucky), shift into a lower gear as if you were coming to a short, steep uphill. Commit to your line and hit the soft stuff with your pedals spinning fast and furious. When both tires are in it, the goopy stuff will grab on to your tires and slow you down. If you shifted into the right gear, you will be able to maintain some of your momentum and spin through. If you're in too big a gear, then you won't be able to spin fast enough to keep the bike moving and a stall and dab will result.

Here are some more tips for soft conditions.

1. Adjust your tire pressure. If conditions are generally soft—if most of the trail is muddy or snowy or sandy—then run your tires about 5 to 10 psi (pounds per square inch, the standard rating of air pressure) lower than you normally would. This will give you better traction for two reasons. One, the lower the pressure the more surface area of the tire is in contact with the trail, giving the bike more "float" since the weight of the rider is distributed over a larger area. Two, a softer tire conforms to the trail more, giving the rider more traction on wet rocks, logs, and so on. Be careful not to let out too much air; an under-inflated tire is prone to flats, as is explained in chapter 4.

2. Keep your weight back. When you're approaching a soft section stand slightly off your seat and get your weight slightly back, as if you were approaching a downhill. Front wheels tend to dig into the soft stuff, resulting in erratic and unpredictable steering. The front tire has to push the sand out of the way in order to track properly. By keeping the front wheel lighter, the tire sinks in less and will track better.

3. Don't trash the trail. Just because there's mud in the trail doesn't mean you should ride through it. While riding through transient patches of mud in the trail owing to rain usually won't cause much damage, riding through year-round bogs and wetlands can upset ecosystems and damage wildlife. Just because there are tire tracks, it doesn't mean you have permission to ride through. When in doubt, walk your bike through or around the mud. Many coastal and arid regions are very sandy—guess how Sand Flats Road in Moab, Utah, got its name. Any vegetation in these areas is fragile, and is responsible for keeping the soil in place. A tire track can cause damage that will take decades to repair itself. Don't leave the trail to get around a soft spot. This is one of the most common and difficult rider problems to control on mountain bike trails. As each rider goes farther off the trail to avoid the soft spot, a wider and wider area becomes chewed up by bike tires. The result is a wide sand pit, or mud bog, and ultimately closed mountain bike trails.

SLICK ROCK

Every serious mountain biker must ride the Slick Rock Trail in Moab at least once in his or her life, or be doomed to wander about in mountain biking purgatory for all eternity. Here's a short guide to securing your spot in mountain bike heaven.

Riding on the Slick Rock Trail is like no other experience in mountain biking. The formations that constitute the rock are actually ancient sand dunes, buried for millions of years, transformed into sandstone, and then exposed by erosion. The undulating terrain is composed totally of sandstone. The terrain is so devoid of soil and vegetation that stripes of paint mark the trail as it winds its way through the lunar landscape. Without the guidance of these stripes you'd be lost in the first five minutes of your ride.

Because of the gritty nature of the rock the traction is almost scary. It's amazing how you can climb slopes that would be impossibly steep with any other kind of trail surface. Slick tires with no tread are best in these conditions. The lugs found on standard mountain bike tires aren't necessary for traction, and have too much rolling resistance on hard surfaces. If you do ride slick rock with regular tires try inflating them to 65 to 80 psi. This will give you much less rolling resistance, allowing you to travel faster with less effort.

The main thing to remember while riding here is that your bike can do much more in this environment than you think. That steep climb up a nearly vertical slope *is* doable. And because the traction is so superior you don't need to worry about weighting the rear tire in the climb. What you *do* need to work on is keeping that front wheel down. I've been so far forward on some of these pitches that when I look down my eyes are forward of the front tire and my handlebars are at mid-thigh level.

The key in descending is also not letting the terrain psych you out. When coming down a super-steep pitch instinct tells you that it's too steep—you'll slide and fall. But because of the rock your tires will hold on to almost anything. Commit to the descent. If you think you may walk down, decide at the top of the pitch and start walking. If you hesitate or try to bail out halfway down you very well may fall. When bare skin and slickrock meet, the rock wins.

When you visit the Slick Rock Trail, don't forget to sign in and drop a donation in the box at the trail head. In 1993 more than 90,000 bikers rode on Slick Rock, straining the resources of the local rescue squad and the Bureau of Land Management. Your donations will go a long way in keeping the entire area open to mountain bikers.

POSITIVE VISUALIZATION

When I try to learn anything—ski jumping, weight lifting, whatever—I have to complete the action myself and see what it feels like to understand it. Once I experience it firsthand, I recognize and capture it. I can't reach that point by chopping the experience up into tiny pieces, the way you would by learning from a diagram.

In the real world, that means you can start improving your riding once you learn to con-

centrate on the results rather than the particulars of your actions. This approach to life might ring a bell. It's called positive visualization, and if you've always considered it a crock, you'll be surprised how much it can affect your biking experience. If you ski, you may have already applied this kind of thinking—and been amazed at the results.

At the top of a highly technical section of trail, for example, I'll look down, consciously pick a line I'm going to follow, and try hard not to analyze it. I don't second-guess myself; I don't study the terrain. I imagine the line down as a flowing curve, not a choppy bunch of segments. I picture an abstract line of movement, not a physical line in the ground; I envision a line in three dimensions, not two, that almost has a distinct geometry.

You'll eventually develop your own visualization mantras. In a climb, I imagine myself as—yes—a mountain goat. I say it over and over to myself: "I am a mountain goat, I am a mountain goat." It blocks doubt from creeping into my consciousness and flushes all negativity out of my brain. All my head does is tell my legs to move. When I reach the top, I eat tin cans.

Just kidding. But try to take this concept seriously. Abstract as it sounds, visualization helps you to a practical, bottom-line goal—focus. It also distracts you from any worries you might have about the trail and eliminates doubt simply by leaving no room for it. It drowns out background noise. It's standard practice in sports to visualize your task completed; you picture a situation so your body knows what to do when it gets there. It won't work every time. It's an ideal, something to reach for. The payoff is that your visualization will actually coincide with the reality every so often.

Use whatever works for you. Uphill, imagine your head's filled with helium or that the starship *Enterprise* is beaming you up to the top. Downhill, imagine yourself as a snake slithering down, or as a fifty-five-gallon drum of water spilling down, or as a skier in deep powder. Your friends might think you've cracked, but who cares? If they can't relate to your creative behavior, you don't want them around, anyway.

Try it right now. Look across the room, pick a point where you'd like to end up, and visualize the line you'll pick to get there. Don't think about the obstacles; if there's a sofa or table in your way you'll just skirt it without thinking. Try it outside; choose a point down the street or in the yard, imagine a line taking you there, and follow it (just look both ways before you cross the street).

In the end, with all the exercises, physics, and psychology, you're aiming for a kind of riding equilibrium where all the concepts we've outlined come together. Ironically, you really reach that state of balance without trying to get there. It's one of the hardest things to teach in mountain biking. More than a skill, it's a state of being. And rather than a discrete goal, it's more like a place you reach. Eventually, you'll develop the instinct that takes you there. You'll fatigue less because you'll stop fighting the terrain. You'll feel a healthy aerobic fatigue instead of muscle soreness. And you'll enter a nonverbal state of being where *doing* replaces *thinking* and everything finally makes perfect sense.

4

······

KING OF THE MOUNTAIN

Trail Selection and Navigation; Backcountry Safety and Repair

CHOOSING TRAILS

After much careful study, I've developed a highly technical definition of what constitutes a "good" mountain biking trail. Ready?

It's anything that's fun to ride. Fun is the most important thing in mountain biking. Think about it. If you're not having fun, what's the point? The state of being that is fun comes from an acceptance, an embracing of the process. You can't have fun with something when you're fighting it or wishing it were somehow different. Were you expecting a more complex theory? Sorry, but to me determining what's good seems a simple issue of interaction between the rider and the trail. What I might find fun may be hell on wheels for someone else, and vice versa.

At the risk of sounding sentimental, the key to discovering the joy of mountain bike terrain is within yourself. Fun is where you make it. To me fun is had in gaining a new experience, having the feeling that I've added a page to my book of life. Some of the best riding I've ever done was in the Everglades during mosquito season. I got eaten alive, but it was something I'd never done before. It was beautiful because it was a complete experience in itself.

Whether you're traveling or just looking for terrain near where you live, the first step to locating enjoyable trails is finding a bike shop with a mountain biking focus. You'll find other riders there who know the territory. Bike shops—and other mountain bikers—can become an invaluable resource and help you bypass a lot of trial and error. Call or visit a bike shop near where you want to ride. I've done this many times and have always found shop employees to be friendly and extremely helpful. Describe what kind of riding you want to do. Discuss hilliness, mileage, degrees of technicality, muddy or dry, single track vs. fire roads. Ask about seasonal considerations: Is it the buggy season? Any monster snakes? What time does it get dark? Is there water available on the trail? Like the old adage says, there are no stupid questions; you'll feel much more stupid when the rescue squad hauls you out of the woods at 3 A.M.

Ask for any maps that are available and where to get them. But bear in mind that while maps can be an essential tool in discovering trails, they're not always reliable. Too often information is out of date, incomplete, or simply incorrect. I've spent too much time in the woods of Vermont, exploring trails that ultimately went nowhere. More than once I've had to backtrack for hours after reaching a dead end where the map clearly showed a connection to another trail.

Sometimes misinformation can lead you to discover a truly magnificent trail. It's taken fifteen years, but I've used my trials and errors to develop my own list of routes in southern Vermont. If you live in an area with an extensive network of trails—and you've got the time—you can develop your own trail system the same way. If you're like most mountain bikers, though, you probably can't afford to waste valuable riding time looking for trails that may or may not be there. That's when your local bike shop can be a lifesaver.

The best places to look for trails are publicly owned lands, either state or federal. Many of those areas are closed to mountain biking, so it's important to be aware of regulations concerning mountain bikes in a particular area. They vary widely from state to state, and even within a particular state.

Take the New York metropolitan area, where I've been spending a lot of time riding the past few years. You might think (as I first did) that the area wouldn't offer much good biking. But New Jersey, especially, has an impressive system of state parks and reserves, many of which are open to mountain bikes. Some parks ban mountain bikes; others officially have bans in place but rarely enforce them. (A ranger told me this, honest!) Many have a policy that allows mountain biking in designated areas, and some have no policy at all. Warning: Many areas don't post regulations on trail heads, so the only way to find out is to ask.

If you can't find areas near you that allow mountain biking, consider organizing. Work together with other riders to convince local officials to open terrain. Don't expect it to be easy; many organizations (who shall remain nameless) out there want to keep us off trails. These groups have been around for a long time, and are very well organized. They're also worth fighting. I feel strongly that public lands are just that: public. We have as much right as anyone to enjoy the backcountry, and it's up to us to earn that right for the future of the sport by acting as goodwill ambassadors, committed to responsible riding and sharing the trail with other users.

Based in Boulder, Colorado, the International Mountain Bicycling Association (IMBA) is dedicated to public education as well as to gaining and preserving access to mountain bike trails. IMBA can provide materials to assist local bike clubs with preventing trail closures and opening new terrain. These folks work hard to protect our rights as mountain bikers. They deserve your support; I urge you and your friends to join. See the listings in Appendix B for details on how to contact the folks at IMBA.

MAP AND COMPASS

To determine what the terrain will look like before you get where you're going, you can get a detailed topographical ("topo") map of virtually any locality in the United States (see Figure 4.1). The U.S. Geological Survey makes them, backcountry outfitters sell them, and they generally won't set you back more than two or three dollars. You can get one of Chicago or Manhattan, as well as rural and suburban locales. Since they make open and developed areas very clear, finding trails can become a lot easier if you check these maps beforehand.

The first step in planning a route is to open up your map and identify the area in which you're going to ride. Lay out the ride as a loop, a point-to-point, or an out-and-back. If you're riding in an area unfamiliar to you, consider setting up your ride as an out-and-back. This way, if anything goes wrong, or if you get lost, you can simply backtrack and return to civilization. Don't forget to make a note of each intersection you pass, so that on your return you know which way to go. It also helps to simply turn around once in a while to see what the terrain looks like going in the other direction. Things look very different when you're traveling in the opposite direction, and this will help you recognize terrain on your return trip. Take a look at the example map on page 70. You'll see the legend in the bottom right-hand corner. This is where you'll find all the informa-

tion you need to read and understand the map.

There are many books on the market that explain, in detail, how to use a map and compass. If you plan on riding on unmarked trails in remote areas, it's worth the effort to become proficient in map and compass use; it could save your life. By using a compass you can determine your location, the location of other features such as mountains, streams, roads, and towns, and your direction of travel. All these things are extremely important while navigating the backcountry.

Once you've found the area to ride in, calculate the distances on your route. Virtually all maps, topographical or not, have a scale. The scale explains the relationship between distances on paper and the real world. Scales are depicted graphically and in ratios. When you see a scale expressed as 1:25,000, that means that 1 inch on the map equals 25,000 inches in the real world. Divide 25,000 by 12 to determine the feet per inch (2,083.33), then by 5,280 to find out how many miles per inch (.39). Mileage can also be estimated by lining a ruler up to the graphic scale and counting out the miles along the route. Expect to average 3 to 5 mph, or even less in rugged terrain.

Next, look at the legend on the map to see what kind of road or trail surfaces you'll encounter along your ride. Most maps use a pair of solid lines to depict paved roads, pairs of dotted lines to depict dirt or gravel roads, and a single dashed line to depict trails. Use these rough guidelines to identify the type of terrain you'll be riding.

When you look at a topographical map you'll see a bunch a squiggly lines going in every direction but never crossing each other.

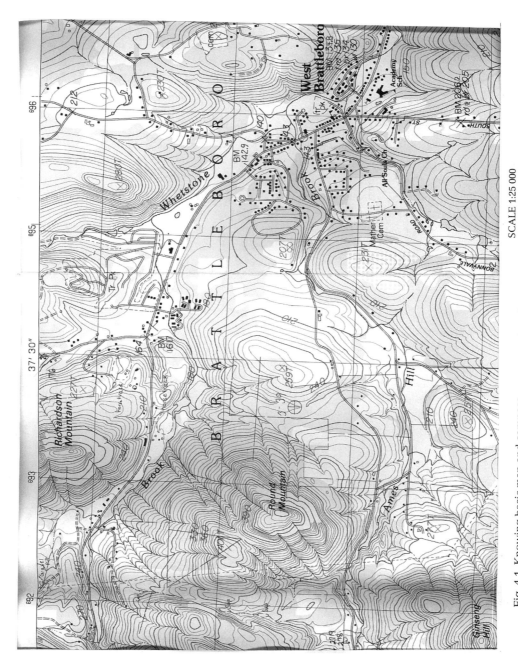

SCALE 1:25 000

1 centimeter on the map represents 250 meters on the ground

CONTOUR INTERVALS 6 METERS

Fig. 4.1. Knowing basic map and compass skills can save your life.

These are contour lines and they designate regular intervals of elevation. Contour lines are useful because they give us a representation of a three-dimensional world expressed in a two-dimensional format. If you walk along one of these lines out in the real world (you can't see them, since they're imaginary) you neither rise nor fall in elevation.

If you change your direction and cross the contour lines, you either gain or lose elevation. The closer together the contour lines, the steeper the terrain; the farther apart, the more gentle the slope. Level areas appear as sections with no lines, or very few lines widely spaced. Contour lines are expressed in increments of either feet or meters. Older maps use feet, newer ones meters. The vertical distance between lines is called the contour interval. Most topographical maps have a contour interval of about 20 feet, or 6 meters. On every fifth line, a number is written. This is the elevation, expressed in feet or meters, of that location. By determining the elevations at different points along the route, you can determine where you'll be climbing and where you'll be descending.

Contour lines help us gauge the difficulty of a ride. The more elevation changes, the more climbing required. Climbing, as we know, is slower and requires more effort than riding on comparatively level terrain. When you see contour lines close together, anticipate steep climbs and descents and a slower travel rate.

Most maps are oriented so that north is at the top of the page, south is at the bottom, west to the left, and east to the right. The compass has the same points of direction, expressing them in degrees. The compass uses 360 degrees, just like in geometry, with north being 360, or 0 degrees, south 180, west 270, and east 90 degrees. Most compasses have a bezel—the part of the compass that holds the needle—mounted on a rotating base. This allows you to move the base in relationship to the needle to determine true north. All the other directions are fixed in relation to north, so they automatically line up properly.

The problem with compass use is that the needle on a compass points at magnetic north, not true north. True north is located exactly at the north pole. Magnetic north, on the other hand, lies to the southwest of true north, somewhere around Hudson Bay, Canada. In order to determine true north you need to know the difference, expressed in degrees of the compass, between true north and magnetic north. On your topo map you'll see a phrase that says something like "magnetic declination 5 degrees E." This is the information you need to determine true north for your location. It's different on each map and in each location around the world, depending on where you are in relation to magnetic north.

Here in Vermont, the magnetic declination is 15 degrees west. That means that magnetic north lies at 15 degrees west of true north, or at 345 degrees. To determine true north lay your compass on a flat surface or hold it as level as possible in your hand. Next, line up the base with the bezel and the red end of the needle so that they all point at the "N" on the bezel. Now rotate the whole thing so that the red end of the needle points at 345 degrees. Remember, the needle always points at magnetic north, and in Vermont magnetic north is at 15 degrees west of true north, or 345 degrees. As long as the red needle points at 345 degrees all the other points of the compass are correct. Now the "N" points at true north, the "S" points due south, and so on.

When you're out on the trail, check your direction by orienting yourself to the points of the compass. Go through the exercise we've just outlined and check the direction you're traveling against the direction on the map. If the trail you're following appears to head east, but the trail on the map leads north, you may have made a wrong turn. If you come to an intersection of trails that are not outlined on the map and you're not sure which way to go (it happens all the time; even the best maps have a degree of inaccuracy), you can check to see in what direction the trail leads. Remember that trails have many twists and turns that may not be accurately depicted on the map, so take several readings to be sure.

If you get lost, backtrack to the best of your ability. Don't, for any reason, leave the trail, or you may become hopelessly lost. If you do lose the trail, immediately backtrack and find it. If the trail peters out and becomes difficult to find, turn around and go back. If you still find yourself lost and are unable to find the trail, use your map and compass to get out of trouble. First, stop where you are and take out your map and compass. Identify the spot where you last knew where you were. Take a look at the map for any landmarks, mountain peaks, or streams that could help you locate yourself.

One bit of advice you may have heard for lost hikers is to walk downhill until you find a stream, and follow the drainage downstream. The thinking is that civilization is usually in val-ley floors, and by following the stream downhill you'll find civilization. This is generally true, but in some areas the stream could lead you farther away from civilization. Check with your map to see where the drainages in the area lead. If you can be sure that following a stream will bring you back to civilization, then go ahead and start making your way.

You can also try using your compass to navigate to a known road or trail. Let's say you can identify the general area in which you are lost. Do this by locating the spot where you last knew where you were and drawing a circle of a couple of miles around it (or however far you think you may have traveled since you were there). This is the area in which you became lost. Next, look for a nearby road or trail, preferably one that has some length to it and is entirely outside the circle you've drawn. Now, using your map, determine in what general direction the road lies. Say the road runs north-south on your map, and the circle you've drawn lies west of the road. By traveling due east from anywhere in that circle, you'll intersect with the road.

Next, use your compass and orient yourself. Find true north and due east. While keeping the needle of the compass pointed at magnetic north, turn the base of the compass and point it east. Pick an object in the distance to your east—a tree or a rock—and walk to it. Repeat until you've reached the road. Look to make sure there are no major obstacles in your path, such as a major river or canyon that cannot be crossed. If you're in thickly wooded terrain, it could take many hours to reach your goal. Leave your bike behind, but take along any

When you're in the backcountry, help is not waiting behind every tree.

food, water, clothing, and medical supplies. If it's getting dark, find a sheltered area and hunker down until morning. A campfire can save your life in the cold air of the mountains, and it'll help searchers spot you from the air (of course, you also let someone know where you were going, right?).

If you've done everything right, you'll never find yourself in this situation. Use common sense and know when to turn back.

COMMON SENSE IN THE BACKCOUNTRY

It's a big world out there, and when you're out in the backcountry, far from civilization, you need to behave as if every decision you make could be a matter of life and death. Whether you're sixty miles out in the desert in Utah or riding in a small state park in Ohio with civilization all around, you need to be thinking, "What will I do if one of us gets hurt?" "Who will I call?" "Where's the nearest phone?"

One of the concepts I learned while training to become an emergency medical technician (EMT) is that of the worst-case scenario. Worst-case scenario means just that: What's the worst thing that could happen? What would you do if someone you're riding with gets hurt and can't ride? What if you have a major breakdown and have to walk out of the woods? Anticipate the worst. By thinking ahead you can mentally prepare for the unexpected.

One of the problems with city people who visit rural areas to mountain bike is that they expect to see a phone booth behind every tree. They don't seem to realize that while one side of a mountain could contain stores, homes, and civilization, the other side may disappear into several hundred thousand acres of wilderness and empty land. Remember what we said in chapter 3 about fear. A healthy amount of fear instills respect for the terrain. Respect for the planet and the outdoors is at the heart of what mountain biking is about. Respect will give you pause and help you make good decisions about where to go and how to behave.

If you're in unfamiliar territory and hit a truly treacherous trail, there's one basic rule: get off and walk. Don't get embarrassed or self-conscious. This is one of the commandments of mountain biking, and even the most fearless, thrill-seeking kamikazes know when a trail's just not safe for their comfort level. We all have an often erroneous instinct that says, "It'll get better right around the corner." It doesn't always get better; as a matter of fact, it often gets worse. Know your limits.

Minor injuries can become life-threatening when you're far from help. Be prepared. A few hours of training and some basic supplies can mean the difference between a happy ending and tragedy. Avoid serious injuries by using your common sense in the backcountry. I encourage everyone to call his or her local ambulance squad or American Red Cross office and sign up for a first-aid course. A basic first-aid course will take about eight hours of your time and will teach you how to handle minor injuries like abrasions, lacerations, and contusions; how to protect yourself and others from contamination by blood-borne diseases; and how to identify more serious injuries that will require you to call for help.

It's beyond the scope of this book to teach first-aid principles; if I tried, I'm sure some of you would feel you'd learned enough and wouldn't bother to take a course. But I strongly believe you have no business being in the backcountry, especially if there are others depending on you, unless you've had at least minimal first-aid training. Take time to invest in your safety and the safety of others.

■ ■ ■

When in doubt—walk!

I remember participating a few years ago in a frantic search-and-rescue mission for a twenty-nine-year-old man and a twelve-year-old boy who went mountain biking and disappeared at Mount Snow. With helicopters circling overhead and bloodhounds combing the woods, the scene looked like something out of an action movie.

The pair had gone out too late, around 4:15 P.M., and were to return for dinner at 5:30. At 2:00 the following afternoon, nearly twenty-four hours later, one of the rescue team found them, some thirty miles from their point of origin. The pair endured a chilly (45-degree), damp Vermont night, during which they could have died of hypothermia. From a safety perspective, they did everything wrong.

There are some basic guidelines everyone should follow before a mountain bike ride anywhere, and especially in *terra incognita:*

1. Know where you're going. Plan the route, and consider how long it will take. When mountain biking, you travel a very slow average of only 3–5 mph, compared to about 10–15 mph with road biking, so keep that in mind when planning a day trip. This ill-fated pair should have realized they couldn't really go anywhere in an hour, anyway.

2. Check in with someone—your local bike shop, your significant other, your next-door neighbor, whomever—and let them know where you plan to go. Even when I can't reach anyone, I provide a record of my trip by leaving a photocopy of the trail map on the kitchen table with my planned route outlined in red, just in case. If people have to search for me, they know what to follow. When the search

parties set out for the man and boy, all we could do was fan out from the point of origin.

3. Never disregard signs. If a route is closed or a signpost warns of a trail off-limits, respect it. Along with protecting yourself, obeying signs is your responsibility to searchers, who might have to risk their own lives to save yours. Just remember that if people have to search for you, you're putting them at risk.

4. Unless you're planning on night riding, figure out when the sun's going to set and leave yourself enough time to make it back before dark.

5. Know what kind of weather you're facing, and prepare yourself.

6. Always take food and water.

7. Carry dry newspaper and waterproof matches or a lighter to build a fire—hypothermia is a danger even in the summer months.

8. Take a first-aid course and always carry first-aid supplies.

Take what you're doing seriously. Always prepare for the worst-case scenario. Too often for too many unprepared riders, the nightmare scenarios come true. Food, matches, newspaper, and an extra layer of clothes can save your life. With all the crazy stunts I do and chances I take on the trail, I'll never push my luck with safety.

BEFORE YOU RIDE— THE QUICK CHECK

The Quick Check is like a routine physical exam for your bike. I devised it in 1988 at the Mount Snow Mountain Bike School to check everyone's bike before we took them out for the day. In the same way a doctor looks for signs of underlying problems in your body, the system lets you examine the trail fitness of your bike.

Make it a habit to conduct the Quick Check before each ride. It won't take long—about thirty seconds to a minute if all is well—but can save much more time and a lot of aggravation on the trail.

1. Check your headset. Lock your front brake. Turn your handlebars 90 degrees. While pushing down on the handlebars, rock your bike back and forth. Listen and feel for any looseness in the bearings of your headset. Next, with one hand, lift your front wheel off the ground and push the handlebars from one side to the other. The fork and front wheel should turn freely without binding. If both of these items check out, your headset is properly adjusted. If a knocking comes from your headset, it needs to be tightened; if the front fork does not turn freely, it needs to be loosened. If your headset is worn out, you won't be able to adjust it perfectly. When you think you've got the right tightness, it'll bind, and when you back it off just a bit it'll knock. Those are the signs your headset is worn out and needs to be replaced.

2. Check your bottom bracket. While leaning over your bike's top tube, grasp one crank arm (not the pedals) in each hand. Try to move the cranks laterally to the bike. If you hear and feel knocking, your bottom bracket may need to be tightened. If your crank arms are loose, you'll hear the same noise; before you start adjusting your bottom bracket, tighten your crank arms and recheck. To inspect your bottom bracket for tightness, slip the chain off the chain rings and spin the cranks. They should spin easily, without noise.

3. Check your wheels. Lift the front wheel off the ground with one hand. Try to move the wheel side to side, laterally to the bike. Once again, listen and feel for looseness in your bearings. Next, spin the wheel and check for any binding. Be sure your brake pads aren't rubbing on the rim; you might mistake this for tight wheel bearings. Repeat for the rear wheel.

Check for wheel trueness. While you spin your wheels, watch as the rim passes through the brake pads. Note any side-to-side wobble. Be sure to look only at the metal part of the rim. Tires will always wobble slightly; this could throw you off into thinking the wheel is out of true. Check that the quick releases on your wheels are clamped properly and secure.

Check your spokes for looseness by squeezing several at a time. Work your way around the wheel and note any loose spokes. Inspect the sidewall of your rim for excessive wear. Worn rims will be cupped inward, a result of abrasion from the brake pads. Worn rims will affect your braking power, since there will be less surface area for the pads to contact. Worn rims can also fail, crumpling under a big impact. Don't let your pads deteriorate to this point; obviously, it makes riding extremely dangerous.

Squeeze your tires, or use a tire gauge, to check their pressure. Depending on your weight, and the conditions wherever you ride, tires should be inflated to 35 to 75 psi.

4. Check your brakes. Combine this step with the wheel check. Spin your wheels and watch the spots where the pads line up with the rim. Some pads, by virtue of their design, tend to work their way toward the sidewall of the tire as they wear. If the pad rubs on your tire it will wear through the very thin material of the sidewall—shredding it, ruining the tire, and giving you a flat that you won't be able to patch on the trail.

Check pads for excessive wear. Don't let your pads wear all the way down to the metal; they'll wreck your rims, and rims will cost a lot more than pads to replace.

Squeeze your brake levers to lock up your brakes and check for cable adjustment. Fine-tune your barrel adjustments for maximum braking power.

5. Check your cables. Look where your brake and shifter cables attach to the derailleurs and brake set. Make sure that the cables are securely fastened at their attachments. Make a note to replace any cables that look frayed or rusted.

6. Check your shifting. Hop on your bike and ride it around the immediate area. Ride up a short steep hill and shift under a load. If you detect any skipping or hesitation in the shift, fine-tune your cable adjustment (as outlined in "Dave's 10-Step Program to Keep Your Bike in Top Running Condition," pages 35–38).

7. Check your chain. Backpedal your cranks. Watch and listen as the chain passes through the rear derailleur. Tight links can seize up and catch in your rear derailleur, breaking it, or can even rip it out of its dropout, ruining the threads and your frame if you don't have replaceable dropouts. You can prevent tight links by keeping your chain clean and well lubed. Tight links will make a clicking

noise as they pass through the jockey pulleys of your rear derailleur. To loosen tight links put a drop of lubricant on the offending link and work it side to side until the pin moves easily. If there are many tight links, or if you can't loosen them, replace the chain.

8. Check everything else. Make sure you're carrying all the tools you may need. (See "Backcountry Repair," below, for a tool list.) Check that your water bottle cages are attached securely, that stem and handlebar bolts are tight, that brake and shifter levers are tightened, and that any mounted packs or bags are zipped and secure.

Following the Quick Check regularly—and addressing problems quickly—will help you avoid many common trailside emergencies.

BACKCOUNTRY REPAIR

Everything we've covered so far has been designed to prepare you for hitting the trail. You've done everything right. You're ready for anything. What could happen? Plenty. No matter how well prepared you think you are, there's always something else that can go wrong. Yes, being prepared will minimize your potential problems on the trail. But not every scenario can be anticipated. The ability to improvise with a simple tool kit is one of the skills a mountain biker needs to master.

When it comes to what to bring on a ride, I have a split personality. On one hand, I believe in a kind of trail minimalism—just the bare essentials. When I ride by myself, I often take just a patch kit, an Allen wrench set, and my pump.

But I tend to go overboard when I'm leading a group, bringing just about the entire bike shop with me. My thinking is, the more bikes, the more things to go wrong. Pack your tool kit according to the length of your ride, the type of terrain, and the size of your group.

Here's a list of tools and replacement parts to bring along on your ride (see Figure 4.2). I've divided the list into three parts: essential, recommended, and optional.

ESSENTIAL

- **Patch kit,** to repair punctures in your tire tubes. These kits contain rubber disks with glue and a little piece of sandpaper. Believe it or not, they do the trick.

- **Tire lever,** to take off the tire in question. Mountain bike tires are much easier to remove from the rim than road tires; you should need only one lever.

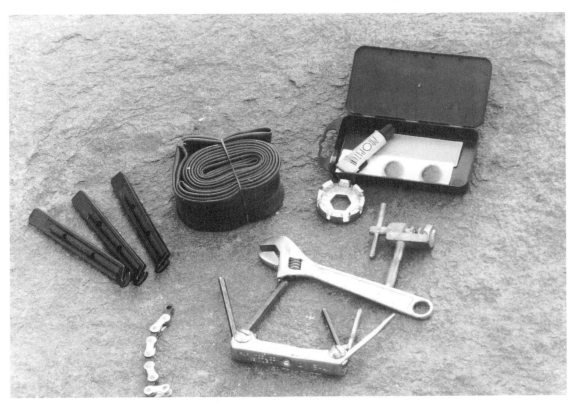

Fig. 4.2. A well-stocked tool kit can mean the difference between fun and disaster.
(Photo by Mike Piniewski)

- **Adjustable wrench, Allen wrench set,** and **Phillips head screwdriver,** which you'll use, trust me, for everything from adjusting derailleurs to tightening water bottle cages. Your local bike shop should carry several combination tools; pick whichever you like best. Headset wrenches, chain tools, Allen wrench sets, and adjustable wrenches are included in one compact, easy-to-carry package.

- **Chain tool,** the only thing between you and a long walk home if you break your chain.

- **Pump,** which you'll be sorry you don't have if you get a flat. I don't recommend CO_2 cartridges, which are one-use-only, disposable items. Though they're much faster than a pump and racers use them frequently, we're not in that much of a hurry.

RECOMMENDED

- **Spare tube,** to speed up the process of fixing a flat considerably; but don't let it replace your patch kit. A tube is good for one flat only, while a patch kit can fix a half-dozen or more.

- **Shifter and brake cables,** one of each. If you bring cables long enough to reach the rear brake or rear derailleur you can also use it on the front by either cutting to length if you have wire snips, or taping the excess cable to your seat or chain stays.

- **Spoke wrench,** to replace or tighten spokes. Ask the folks down at the bike shop for a multisize one. These look like little chrome doughnuts with notches cut out of them.

They're not much bigger than a single-size wrench, and having a multisize spoke wrench will allow you to help out others who may have different size spoke nipples.

- **Cloth medical tape,** for anything from fixing a blown-out shoe to a shredded tire sidewall.

- **Jackknife,** for trimming worn brake pads and spreading peanut butter, among other things.

- **Butane lighter,** to start a fire in case of emergency.

- **Small flashlight,** a lifesaver if you get caught out after dark.

OPTIONAL

- **Spare rear derailleur,** because, in Vermont, it seems there's always a stick ready to jump out and break your rear derailleur. Every season, I replace at least two rear derailleurs while I'm actually out on the trail. While there are things you can do if yours becomes dysfunctional (see "The Four Most Common Trailside Breakdowns and How to Fix Them" for details), having a spare is the best option. If you live in an area without a lot of brush and sticks in the trail, you can leave it at home.

- **Spare chain links,** because if you break your chain, or need to remove a section of your chain, some spare links can save you from having to overshorten your chain, which can adversely affect shifting. You'll find spare chain links at your local bike shop;

I'm sure they have more than they know what to do with.

- **Extra spokes,** which you can tape to your chain stays. If you break a spoke, you can replace it using your spoke wrench. Not all spokes are created equal; you'll find dozens of lengths and gauges to accommodate different rims and hubs. Check with your local bike shop to make sure you have two or three of the right size replacement spokes.

THE FOUR MOST COMMON TRAILSIDE BREAKDOWNS AND HOW TO FIX THEM

FLAT TIRE

There are two main causes of flats: thorns or other sharp objects, and pinch flats. Pinch flats occur when the tube is squished between the rim and a blunt object in the trail. Pinch flats can happen anytime, but are most common when the tire is underinflated. This type of flat is also known as a "snakebite" because of the signature double puncture marks left on the tube by the sidewalls of the rim.

The first step in fixing a flat is to identify the cause and locate the puncture. Start by loosening the quick release and removing the offending wheel. Next, use your tire lever to pry the bead (the part of the tire that fits onto the rim) off the rim. Slide the lever around the rim to separate the bead from the rim. Remove one bead only; it's not necessary to completely remove the tire from the rim. If the tube has a presta valve (the long, skinny kind with a knurled brass nipple at the end) unthread the small metal fastener that holds the valve in place.

Before you remove the tube, place the wheel in front of you with the valve at 180 degrees, or 12 o'clock. Remove the tube, setting it aside with the same orientation: right side up, with the valve at 12 o'clock. Carefully run your fingers around the inside of the tire, feeling for thorns or glass that may have pierced the tire. Inspect the inside of the rim to see if your rim strip (the strip of rubber that protects the tube from the spoke heads) is torn or has slipped, or if a broken spoke has worked its way up into the rim and punctured the tube. Inspect the sidewalls of your tire for cuts or abrasions that could cause a flat. Look at the tread pattern of the tire for any protruding foreign objects.

If you find a thorn, a piece of glass, or anything else, note its location using 12 o'clock as your reference. If the thorn was found at 3 o'clock on the tire, then look for the puncture at the corresponding spot on the tube. You can skip the orienting of the tire and tube if you're fixing the flat by replacing the punctured tube with a new one. But it's still important to identify the problem so you can correct it. If you don't remove a thorn when the new tube goes in, you'll get another flat.

If your inspection hasn't turned up anything (you could have a pinch flat, or a thorn could have punctured the tube but not lodged in the tire), inflate the tube until it doubles in circumference. Rotate the tube close to your ear, and listen and feel for air escaping. If there's water nearby, submerge the tube and look for air bubbles. Be sure to check the valve to see if it's stuck or faulty.

Once you've identified and corrected the

problem, either replace the tube and inflate the new one, or patch the damaged tube. To patch a tube make sure it is as clean and dry as possible. Most patch kits have several small round patches and one or two larger oblong patches. Choose whichever best fits the puncture size. Using the piece of sandpaper in the kit, rough up an area on the tube slightly larger than the patch, keeping the hole at the center. Next, apply a thin coat of glue onto the area, spreading it with a tire lever or your jackknife. Don't use your finger; the oils in your skin will keep the patch from adhering to the glue. Allow the glue to dry *before* you apply the patch to the tube. This is the most common mistake riders make while patching tubes. If the glue does not dry so it is tacky but no longer wet, the patch will not hold.

Apply the patch to the tube by peeling the backing off the patch. While making sure you don't touch the contact surfaces, firmly press the patch onto the tube and rub with a rounded object like the back of your tire lever or a closed jackknife. If you've done it right, the patch will lay flat on the tube without the edges peeling up, and without any movement of the patch on the tube.

Before you put the tube back in the tire, make sure the inside of the tire is clean and free of debris, sticks, or sand. Inflate the tube slightly and insert the valve through the hole in the rim while tucking the tube back into the tire. This time, place the valve at 6 o'clock and replace the bead with your fingers, starting at 6 o'clock and working in *both* directions until the bead is back on the rim and your fingers are at 12 o'clock. This will prevent the tube from slipping inside the tire, which can put

pressure on the valve—and cause another flat.

Avoid using tire levers to replace the bead on the rim. This can pinch the tube between the lever and the rim, causing—you guessed it—another flat. Replacing the bead on a narrow rim can be difficult and might even cause you to break a nail, but with persistence you'll get it. If you do have difficulty getting the bead back on the rim use your lever to *carefully* push the bead back onto the rim, making sure the tube is not between the bead and the rim. After you've inflated the tire, check to see that the bead on both sides is seated onto the rim evenly, without any gaps. Check tire pressure with your gauge or simply press the tread with your thumb.

BROKEN CHAIN

Most often, chains break because a tight link binds while under a heavy load. A chain can also break when one or more of its pins torque out of the adjoining link. A broken chain will stop you dead in your tracks, unless you're prepared to fix it.

Take a look at the spare links in your tool kit. You'll see that a bike chain is a series of links that fit between alternating pairs of plates. Each pair of plates is attached to the links at both ends with pins. The chain is flexible because the links and plates pivot on these pins.

When a link ceases to pivot, the chain loses flexibility. A tight link is a weak link, and we all know the old chestnut about chains being only as strong as their weakest link. When a chain has a tight link it fails to distribute its load evenly. This tends to concentrate much of the torque in the area of the tight link. This added

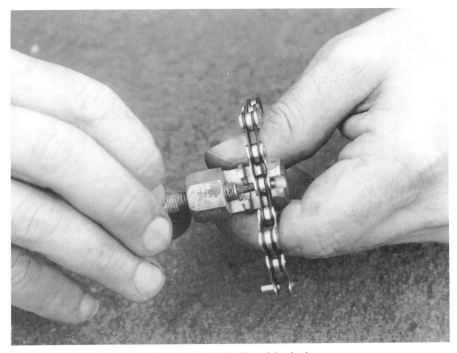

Fig. 4.3. With practice, repairing your chain is no big deal.
(*Photo by Mike Piniewski*)

stress, combined with a lack of flexibility, exerts lateral forces on the chain. Since bike chains were not designed to take lateral stress, the pin torques out of the plate and the chain breaks as a result. To fix a broken chain you need to remove the damaged links and plates and either shorten the chain or replace them with the spares you brought along. (Told you they'd come in handy!)

First, inspect the chain and determine how many links are damaged. It's the plates that are usually bent by the pins as they rip out. When you've decided how many links have to go, re-

move them by pushing the pins through the links with your chain tool (see Figure 4.3).

The chain tool is designed to hold one link while a pin the same size as the one in the chain pushes that pin partly out of the chain (see Figure 4.4). The link is then removed by flexing the chain sideways, which snaps it off. Warning: Don't push the pin all the way out. You'll never, ever get it back in, and you'll have to snap off another link to fix your chain. The pin should protrude slightly on the inside surface of the plate so that when you snap it back together, the link will seat onto the pin, holding it in

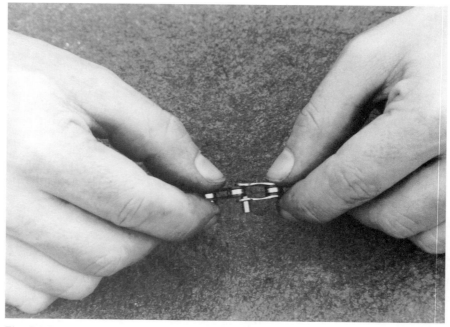

Fig. 4.4. Remember not to push the pin all the way through, so you can snap the links back together. *(Photo by Mike Piniewski)*

place. Make sure you remove the right pin so you are connecting a plate to a link and not a plate to a plate or a link to a link.

Rejoin the chain by snapping the ends back together and pushing the pin back into place with the chain tool. Line up the pin in the chain with the pin in the chain tool and gently push the pin back into place. It's important to line up the pin with the links and plates. You should be able to push the pin back in fairly easily, without straining much. The pin can catch the edge of a plate; if you try to force it, it will bend the plate, and you'll have to start again.

If you don't have spare links with you, it's OK to shorten the chain by as many as five links or so without affecting performance. Much more than that and you'll have trouble getting into some of your gears. That's when adding some links can make a big difference.

Practice while you're watching *Oprah*. Take links apart over and over again until you get the feel for it. On the trail, each mistake results in a shorter and shorter chain. Get it right the first time.

Broken Spoke, Wheel Out of True

Remember what we said in chapter 2 about the strength of the wheel coming from the balanced tension of opposing spokes? Breaking or damaging a spoke can upset this balance and knock the wheel out of true. Spokes can break because of objects caught in your wheel, from crashes, or just from ordinary use and abuse.

If you've broken a spoke but your wheel isn't too warped—if it has no problems fitting through the brake pads—you can probably get away with waiting to fix it. If, on the other hand, the rim is hitting the brake pads, you'll need to use your spoke wrench to get the wheel as close to true as possible.

If you have a spare spoke, replace the broken one by removing the wheel from the frame. Next, deflate the tube, remove the tube and tire entirely from the rim, and peel off the rim strip. Recessed into the rim you'll see a slotted screw head. This is the spoke head that receives the threaded end of the spoke. Unthread the spoke head with your screwdriver, and set it aside. (Make sure you don't drop it in the leaves!) You'll notice the other end of the spoke is bent at a 90-degree angle where it fits into the hub. Push the spoke toward the hub and remove it.

Lace the new spoke through the hub and thread into the reseated spoke head. Then, using your spoke wrench, tighten the spoke just enough to take up the slack. Replace the rim strip, tire, and tube. Inflate the tire, and put the wheel back on the bike. Tighten the new spoke and any others that need it, truing the wheel as outlined in "Dave's 10-Step Program to Keep Your Bike in Top Running Condition," pages 35–38.

Even without a spare spoke, you can still get the wheel reasonably true by tightening several spokes to compensate for the broken one. The more broken spokes, the more difficult this becomes, so do the best you can. First, snip the broken spoke close to the nipple with some wire cutters and slip it out of the hub, or just wrap it around an adjacent spoke to keep it out of the way. Leave the spoke head and nipple in place on the rim. Tighten the two spokes on each side of the broken one, originating from the same side of the hub, a half turn and spin the wheel. Continue to tighten a half turn each until the rim passes easily through the brake pads. We're not looking for perfection here, just a wheel that will get you home. Don't overdo it; the excess tension could snap more spokes, leaving you in deep doo-doo.

Of course, wheels can, and will, come out of true just from routine pounding. By carrying a spoke wrench in your tool kit, you can make adjustments out on the trail, solving small problems before they become major. Sometimes a wheel can become so badly "tacoed," meaning it's acquired the shape of a fried corn tortilla, that no amount of spoke tightening will fix it. In this case you may have to undo your brake quick release so that the wheel can fit through and very carefully (since you're now minus one brake) wobble your way home. This problem seems to plague large people most, since all that weight puts extra stress on the wheels. In extreme cases I've had to take the wheel off the bike and pound it on the ground to make it fit through the chain stays. Needless to say, you'll need to look for a new wheel at that point.

BROKEN OR OUT-OF-ADJUSTMENT REAR DERAILLEUR

Since rear derailleurs are mounted low to the ground, they're extremely vulnerable to damage from sticks, rocks, and any other debris on the trail. Common problems can include anything from slightly bent to completely destroyed derailleurs and hangers.

A damaged rear derailleur will make itself known by failing to shift properly. It'll hesitate, pop and sputter, skip gears, and shift by itself, or it simply won't work at all. Sometimes you won't even be aware that something has happened. A small stick caught in the spokes can catch the derailleur cage and bend it just enough to keep it from working properly. A big stick can actually catch the derailleur cage and rip the derailleur out of its mounting threads (a.k.a. dropout), ruining the frame, your ride, and your day. Aluminum frame bikes have especially delicate threads that are easily damaged. Luckily, most manufacturers have outfitted aluminum bikes with replaceable dropouts, which allow you to fix a $35 part rather than replace the entire frame.

If you think there's something caught in your rear derailleur, stop immediately and clear it before it causes damage. If while riding you feel a little resistance from your rear wheel, your instinct may be to bear down and push harder. Unfortunately, in this case, that could be a mistake that could cost you several hundred dollars. While bike manufacturers warrant their frames, most will consider this type of damage "abuse" and will not cover it. For this reason, I strongly recommend against buying any aluminum or composite frame bike that does not have a replaceable derailleur hanger.

I categorize derailleur damage in two degrees: minor and catastrophic.

Minor derailleur damage usually consists of a slightly bent derailleur cage or hanger. Just letting your bike drop to the ground derailleur-side down can cause it. Tight chain links can also catch in the derailleur cage and produce some minor bending.

For the bike to shift smoothly the chain must align perfectly with the rear cogs. When the hanger or derailleur cage is bent, the chain approaches the rear gears at an angle. This could result in skipping, mis-shifting, and "ghost" shifting. If your bike starts behaving this way, stop for a moment and see if there's any grass or other debris caught in your rear gear cluster. If there is, clean it out and try again. If your gear cluster is free of debris but the bike's still misbehaving, look down the length of your bike from the rear. Align the rear derailleur, chain, and rear gear cluster in your sight line. All three should line up. The derailleur cage should sit straight up and down, not pushed in toward the spokes or pulled out away from them. Look at the derailleur hanger; it should extend from the frame in the same flat plane. Even the slightest deviation can cause major shifting problems. (Your mechanic, of course, has a special tool to diagnose and repair bent hangers, but she's at the shop listening to the Grateful Dead and repacking your kid's tricycle wheels, so what good does that do you?)

If you think the derailleur cage is bent, gently pull or push it back into alignment by grasping it at the bottom jockey pulley. If it looks like the hanger itself is bent, try inserting your 6-mm Allen wrench into the derailleur mounting bolt; while pressing in firmly, use the wrench as a lever to straighten the hanger. Check again and make sure it all works. It's not likely it'll work perfectly, but it can be a big help in serious cases. When you get back to the shop you can have your friendly mechanic straighten everything out for you.

Catastrophic derailleur damage occurs when the derailleur and/or hanger is bent or damaged to the point of nonfunctionality—in other words, broken. A couple of scenarios can help illustrate how a rear derailleur can break:

The stick. You're riding along and there's a stick lying across the trail. When your rear wheel runs over the stick, it pops it into the air and one end gets caught in the spokes. As the wheel turns, the stick goes along for the ride, rotating along with the wheel. Then (this is the bad part), the stick reaches the derailleur cage and catches it, forcing it to rotate back in the direction of the rotation of the wheel. When the derailleur cage gets forced all the way toward the back of the frame, it either snaps the cast aluminum in the main body of the derailleur or rips the mounting bolt out of the dropout, whichever is the weakest part of the assembly.

The chain. A stiff chain link can also break a rear derailleur. The setup: a tight link, or series of tight links, passes through the jockey pulleys. The tight links don't flex and pass through the pulleys, but instead get caught in the cage, forcing the derailleur cage to rotate backward. Result: a mangled rear derailleur.

If the derailleur's trashed but the hanger looks OK, you can either replace the derailleur with your spare (which of course you remembered to bring) or remove it, shorten the chain, and make a 1-speed bike.

To replace the derailleur, shift both your front and rear derailleurs to their smallest cogs. Detach the cable from the derailleur using your 4-mm Allen wrench. If the cable end isn't frayed, and will thread through the new derailleur easily, leave it in place. If the cable end is frayed, remove the cable entirely, pulling it out of the cable housing from the shifter. Next, using your chain tool, separate the ends of the chain and remove it from the jockey pulleys. Now remove the derailleur by loosening its mounting bolt with your 6-mm Allen wrench.

Install the new derailleur by threading it carefully into the hanger threads. Make sure that the tiny set screw near the mounting bolt lines up with the tab on the back of the hanger. Reunite the ends of your chain, being careful to thread the chain properly through the jockey pulleys. Reattach the cable, or install a new one by inserting the cable end at the shifter and working your way to the derailleur, passing the cable through its housing. Before you cinch the cable down, make sure that the chain is on the inner chain ring up front and on the smallest cog in the rear, and that your shifters are also set at this combination. Then, pulling the slack out of the cable with your fingers, tighten the cable attachment at your rear derailleur with your 4-mm Allen wrench. Next, adjust the cable tension, using your barrel adjusters as outlined in "Dave's 10-Step Program to Keep Your Bike in Top Running Condition," pages 35–38.

Before you ride off into the sunset, it's a good idea to set the limit screws of a newly installed rear derailleur. The limit screws are found on the back of the main body of the derailleur. There are two screws, one above the other. These adjusting screws serve to limit the range of motion of the derailleur. The top screw is the high gear adjuster and keeps the chain from jumping off the gear cluster on the outside (your high gear). The bottom screw is the low adjuster and keeps the chain from jumping off the inside of the cluster (low gear).

To adjust the low adjuster shift your chain into the middle chain ring up front and to the largest cog in the back (low gear). You'll notice how the top jockey pulley lines up with the inside cog. The inside edge (toward the spokes) of the jockey pulley should line up with the outside edge (away from the spokes) of the cog. Tighten the bottom limiting screw to pull the derailleur toward the outside, and loosen it to adjust it toward the spokes. Adjust high gear by shifting the chain to the smallest cog, or highest gear, and aligning the inside edge of the top jockey pulley with the outside edge of the smallest cog. Expect to stop occasionally when the chain overshifts, in order to fine-tune the adjustment.

If you don't have a spare rear derailleur, or if the dropout threads are so badly mangled that you can't install one, you still have a chance at riding home by transforming your bike into a 1-speed. Remove the rear derailleur as described, making sure that you stash any loose parts (cables, derailleur, housing, etc.) in your tool kit. Once you're rid of the derailleur and extraneous parts, place your chain, by hand, on the middle chain ring up front and somewhere toward the center of your rear gear cluster. This will give you a middle-of-the-road gear combination—not so big a gear that you can't make it up hills but not so small that you spin excessively on the flats. Look down the length of your bike and see how the chain lines up in relation to the frame. You want the chain placement to be as close to parallel to the frame as possible.

When you think you have a gear combination in as straight a line as possible, loosen the rear wheel quick release and push the wheel to the front of the bike about 1 inch. Take the overlapping ends of the chain and pull them together. Shorten the chain by lining up two ends that will go together and removing the unnecessary section of chain. Close the chain into a loop and then pull the wheel back into its dropout to take up the slack.

Congratulations—you now have a 1-speed bike. If you got the chain in a straight line it should work well without skipping. If the chain has any angle at all, it will try to shift by itself. A gear change will result in either a too tight or too loose chain. Since the rear derailleur is gone, it can't perform its chain tensioning function. A chain that has too much slack will skip, especially when you try to pedal uphill, and a chain that's too tight may break.

One product on the market can actually prevent broken rear derailleurs and blown-out derailleur hangers. Called a breakaway derailleur mounting bolt, it's made out of hollow aluminum and breaks easily. The idea is to make this the weak link in the derailleur assembly. When a stick or chain link gets caught in the derailleur, the mounting bolt snaps, saving your derailleur and hanger. All you need to do is replace the bolt. I've used these bolts with great success for years and recommend them highly; ask your friendly neighborhood mechanic for details.

5

. . . . .

HOW MUCH IS THAT HUFFY IN THE WINDOW?

Buying a Mountain Bike, Accessories, and Components

Never mind hills and rocks—for most people, the most daunting part of mountain biking comes before they hit the trail. Buying a mountain bike can turn the most intrepid consumer into jelly. Can you trust the dealer? Are you getting quality components? If you want to save money, which features can you afford to cut?

Fear not. One simple rule can help answer all these questions before you start looking— and save you time and headaches in the long run: before you begin browsing for a bike, shop for a shop.

Without a doubt, this is the most important—and neglected—step in purchasing a bike. Ask around and try to compile a list of reputable shops. Talk to bikers you know; if you don't know any, find a local bike club and speak to them. A good shop will boast a strong service reputation. It's critical to find a shop that will stand behind its product—and its work—and has personnel who know what

they're doing. You can find shops and then look for bikes in your price range, or you can pick a bike in your price range and then find dependable shops that carry it.

Even if you never see the dealer again after you buy your bike, this is important. Many people aren't aware that most bikes have frames built in Taiwan, and are partly assembled in this country—almost universally in a sloppy fashion. So virtually all dealers, including my bike shop at Mount Snow, take the bike completely apart and rebuild it from scratch, making sure everything's perfect—bearing adjustments, grease in the bearings, and so on.

Every year, when we receive our new rental fleet at Mount Snow, we get sixty-five bikes from a respected manufacturer. Inevitably, half the bearings are too tight, and some of the bikes have no grease in the bearings at all. With virtually no exceptions, there's always a problem when bikes come off the assembly line. So a good bike shop will automatically as-

When it comes to bike shops, bigger is not always better.

sume that any assembly-line bike is bad and start over from the beginning. They end up giving you a bike that's well put together and properly adjusted. If a bike shop simply takes the pieces out of the box and finishes assem-

bling it, you may end up with all kinds of problems that could cost you more money down the road.

Unfortunately, many first-time buyers comparison-shop based on price only. But like a cheap car, a bike deal could turn out to be a lemon. It's critical to ask what the bike shop does to bikes once they get them out of the box. Find out how they put them together. Make sure they tell you they check everything, from the bearings to the brake pads. Don't feel shy or embarrassed; it's your money. Don't take attitude; if they hedge, go elsewhere. A lapse in judgment could cost you a fortune later.

Once you get good answers from two or three shops, you can finally start comparing prices. While I've said it should never become a determining factor in any bike purchase, price is obviously important. Decide on a price range and stick with it, but be realistic. If you've set your spending limit at $200, I suggest waiting a few more months to save up for a decent bike instead.

In general, a serviceable mountain bike starts at around $350 or $400. If that sounds steep, you can find bottom-range bargains by shopping at certain times of year. Scout bike shops in late summer and early fall for deals; that's when they usually need room for new models. And don't assume a bike's defective if it's discounted; the shop may just want to get rid of it. At the shop at Mount Snow, I have to offer 30 percent off some extraordinary bikes simply because it's time to clear them out for new ones.

A friendly caveat: Though I've been known to haggle furiously with salespeople almost anywhere, I'd suggest restraint when it comes to bargaining with bicycle dealers. The markup on new bikes is minuscule, and most dealers make more money off accessories. A bike also represents a considerable labor investment, since the shop has to take it apart

and reassemble it. So try to keep your expectations on price realistic.

Now that you've zeroed in on a shop and a budget, you need to decide which genre of mountain bike suits you. If you thought mountain bikes came in just one flavor, surprise; there are four main food groups, each with very different applications and specs. Except for cross bikes, there are no concrete rules about who can ride what.

Think about what kind of riding you're going to do before you buy. Is your area rocky or sandy? Mountainous or flat? Do you plan on racing, riding in the backcountry, or sticking to fire roads? All these considerations are important when choosing a bike. The more you know about what you want, the better a decision you can make in the store.

TYPES OF BIKES

CROSS, OR HYBRID, BIKES

A cross, or hybrid, bike, is just that—half mountain bike, half road bike. You'll find skinny road-type tires with knobby treads, touring bike frame geometry with flat handlebars, and mountain bike gearing and components.

This is the one for you if (1) you really want to spend most of your time on paved or fire roads but (2) you don't like racing bike handlebars or geometry, and (3) you like mountain bikes for the posture they let you maintain. At one time a very hot category, these bikes were touted as the machines that could handle everything. But, as the saying goes—Jack of all

Cross, or hybrid, bike
(Photo courtesy Specialized Bicycle Components)

trades, master of none. Considering they were created for a perceived market segment rather than a real need, it's not surprising.

Mountain bikes are also known as all-terrain bicycles (ATBs). A real mountain bike is designed for the trail, but it will also do quite well on the road. It won't go as fast as a road bike, but it'll do fine, especially if you pump up the tires a bit. A cross bike, on the other hand, isn't really any better on pavement than a mountain bike and can handle only the tamest of trails. And since most hybrids are targeted at an entry-level market, the components aren't up to the abuse that they'll face on the trail.

My advice to anyone contemplating a cross bike is to first decide if you want to be a mountain biker or a road biker.

RIGID-FRAME BIKES

The real thing. A rigid frame is a good choice if you're serious about mountain biking and want to get started on terrain that's not particularly rocky or rough. For the money, you'll get a nice-looking, versatile bike. If you've considered spending money on a suspension system, consider this first: Bike companies have marketed suspension as the ultimate accessory, and consumers are falling for it hard. But suspension can account for a huge part of a bike's price—and many times it's simply not justified. If you're on any kind of budget, you'll probably have to skimp on components, which I don't recommend. A lot of people who overspend on suspension could do very well with rigid-frame bikes. For an insane rider like me, suspension's essential; for an occasional, not-too-aggressive rider, there's no reason to pay for suspension unless you're really hoping to impress people.

When a customer asks me what kind of bike to get when starting out, I usually recommend a rigid-frame bike. Rather than a bike with all the bells and whistles, the basic rigid-frame bike with a mid- to high-end component group serves as a good starting point. You can get a high-quality rigid-frame bike for around $450. This will get you a steel-frame bike with a solid component group. After you've spent a year or so riding, you'll learn a ton about bikes and riding. You'll be better educated about what kind of bike you'll want when and if you upgrade. On the other hand, you might find that a rigid frame suits you fine and that you'll add some accessories to upgrade your existing bike.

Rigid-frame bike
(*Photo courtesy Specialized Bicycle Components*)

FRONT-SUSPENSION BIKES

Anyone who shares my taste for extreme riding on the gnarliest trails—lots of rocks, roots, serious downhills—will probably also share the need for a suspension bike. If I could own only one bike, I'd choose a front-suspension system. You'll find two basic systems (described in detail in chapter 2): air-oil shocks and elastomer.

Elastomer shocks tend to work well in high-speed situations with a lot of high-frequency vibration, like fire roads with a loose gravel surface and fast, smooth single track. This is be-cause the plastic in the bumpers does a better job damping the vibration than an air-oil shock. Air-oil, on the other hand, does a better job at taking the big hits, such as log jumping and big rocks. It's designed to have a smoother compression phase and rebounds more smoothly because of the oil forced through its valve.

The hottest fork on the market has a combination elastomer and air-oil design. The elastomer bumpers are designed to have an air-oil cartridge inserted inside them. This combination design gives the rider the best of both worlds: superior damping and the ability to handle the big stuff.

Front-suspension bike
(Photo courtesy Specialized Bicycle Components)

FULLY SUSPENDED BIKES

Full-suspension bikes are downhill machines. They're excellent—and essential—for downhill racing, offering the ability to adjust your front and rear wheels to the terrain. Fully suspended bikes are typically much heavier—by three or four pounds—than comparable front-suspension bikes, with some high-tech (but very expensive) exceptions. As you shop, you'll discover there's generally an inversely proportional relationship between weight and cost. A caveat: even for experts, this category can get pretty confusing. The technology's still in flux,

and several companies are still competing to develop the ideal rear suspension system, so shop carefully.

FITTING A BIKE

Once you've decided on price and type, you're ready to fit a bike. Fitting looks easy: hop on, make sure your feet touch the ground, and pedal off into the sunset. In reality, there's much more involved, and you'll want to keep the following factors in mind. Of course, your own comfort should always serve as the ultimate reference point.

Fully suspended bike
(Photo courtesy Specialized Bicycle Components)

STANDOVER HEIGHT

When it comes to fitting a bike, size *is* everything. The paramount consideration is *standover height,* the distance between your crotch and the top tube. You'll want at least 2 inches of clearance when you're standing over the top tube with your feet flat on the ground (you'll need this clearance in case you ever have to make an emergency dismount). The frame should also be small enough to allow you to maneuver your body whenever, wherever, and however you need. Remember how much body movement comes into play when you ride—weight back in the downhill, forward while climbing, all over on technical trails. A big frame will interfere with your transitions, restrict movement, and inhibit your ability to react to terrain; a too-small frame will scrunch you up, arch your back, and cause lower back pain (and make you look like a circus bear on a tricycle to boot).

Keep in mind that one manufacturer's 18-inch frame may not be the same size as another manufacturer's 18-inch frame. You'll notice variations in how the frame is constructed and measured. Fit each bike to your body in person. Don't assume that because one manufacturer's bike is the right size that another with the same listed size will also fit.

TOP TUBE LENGTH

The length of the top tube determines your stretch, or the reach you have on a bike. When the distance is right, your shoulders should be about ten inches to the rear of the handlebars when you're sitting in a comfortable riding position, arms relaxed and extended with a slight bend in the elbows. If you look at your front quick release and hub from a riding position, your handlebars should appear to be forward of them. Bikes come in standard lengths, like shoe sizes, unless you order a custom job. But you can make the stem length longer or shorter, and you can move your seat forward or backward. Since women are typically shorter in the torso, they need shorter frames; unfortunately, most frames are designed for men.

Top tube length often varies among manufacturers, or even among models of the same manufacturer. I'm six feet with a 30-inch inseam. This means I have short legs and a long torso. For years, I rode a bike that was too short for me. I had chronic lower back pain when I rode. I couldn't figure out what I was doing wrong. I stretched and went to the gym to do back exercises, but nothing seemed to work. One day, I was riding with a friend who owned a shop. He pulled up alongside of me and said, "You're all scrunched up on that bike; you need more reach." I looked down and saw he was right—the handlebars were at chest level when I rode low, and my front hub was well forward of my forks.

I experimented with a longer stem, but that created more problems. I was too far over my front wheel and felt insecure in the downhill. I tried moving my seat back, but this affected my pedal stroke. I finally decided to sell my bike and look for one with a longer top tube. I found a bike that had a top tube 1 inch longer than the bike I had been riding—and it made all the

A bike that fits well means a happy rider.

difference in the world. My back pain went away, and as of this writing has not returned.

SEAT HEIGHT

If the seat's at a proper height, your knee should bend slightly when you're sitting in the saddle, and your foot is at the bottom of the pedal stroke with your ankle relaxed and the ball of the foot resting on the pedal. If your seat is too high, you'll have to reach on the down stroke, causing your pelvis to dip toward that side; if the seat's too low, it will push your pelvis up at the top of the pedal stroke. If you ride with the seat too low it can also put undue strain on the quadriceps muscles of your upper thighs. You want it to stay somewhere in between, where you've got an even pedal stroke and your pelvis stays square to the bike while you pedal. Extraneous movement is inefficient and causes muscle fatigue, making riding a literal pain.

FORE AND AFT SEAT ADJUSTMENT

Underneath your seat are two rails to which the seat post attaches. You can loosen a bolt to adjust the seat's forward and back position, which affects your handlebar reach and pedal stroke. In mid-pedal stroke, there should be an imaginary straight line from your knee through the center of the pedal on your forward foot.

The goal is to turn your pedal stroke into a smooth up-and-down motion. Your legs should be like pistons moving straight up and down. If your fore-and-aft adjustment is not correct, you'll have to reach for the pedal in the down stroke; if you're too far back or too far forward, your foot will be behind you at the bottom of the pedal stroke. Either way, your pedaling will become awkward and inefficient.

WOMEN'S BIKES

Women may have a harder time finding both a shop and a bike they trust. Though the sport itself has become a lot more sensitive, female riders still can't get most bike manufacturers to acknowledge they exist.

So-called unisex frames are usually made just for one sex—male. Women are simply expected to adapt. But females typically have proportionally longer legs and shorter torsos than men, so the distance from seat to handlebars is too long for them on many bikes. Women also tend to need smaller bikes than men, sometimes as small as a 13- or 14-inch frame. Most companies make only kids' bikes in these sizes. Kids' bikes are usually inexpensive, heavy, and thrown together with crappy components—not a good choice for a serious, albeit small, adult.

Women's frames (also known as Mixte frames) that you do see on the market are not trail-worthy mountain bikes. Old-fashioned "girls' bikes" are a thing of the past and were designed so that girls' skirts wouldn't bunch up on the top tube—not exactly a concern for the mountain biking woman of the nineties. Women don't need special frame designs, they need bikes proportioned to the female anatomy.

A few companies make small (13-, 14-, and

16-inch) frames that work well for women. Georgina Terry designs an entire line of bikes especially to meet the needs of women riders. Her production volume is low, so prices tend to be high. But if you want a perfect fit, this is your best chance. Barracuda makes a 14-inch aluminum frame bike without a top tube; it has a massive, oversized down tube instead. I've known several women who've done very well with this bike.

Women also need special seats. Since women's pelvises tend to be slightly wider, their ischial tuberosities—better known as butt bones—are positioned wider apart. It's your ischial tuberosity that rests on the seat. The flared portion at the back of the seat is designed to line up with the pelvis. A regular bike seat, one designed for men, is too narrow for women; instead of resting on the bones of the pelvis, women end up riding on the perineum, the skin between the legs. It's not dangerous, but it hurts like hell. Women's seats are designed to be wider, so that the ischial tuberosities rest on the seat, supporting the rider's weight and making for a more enjoyable experience.

I'm convinced that if more bikes were fitted with anatomically correct seats for women, there'd be a lot more women mountain bikers. There's virtual parity at the pro level, but the number of women in recreational riding shrink. We can only hope that as the sport grows, and manufacturers become aware of a lucrative market segment they're missing, these figures will change.

BUYING A USED BIKE

If you want a real bargain, buying a used bike can be the answer. But if you're not careful, it can become a nightmare. Buying a used bike requires more knowledge and wariness to avoid inheriting someone else's headaches. *Caveat emptor,* as those ancient Roman bikers used to say. Before buying a used bike, educate yourself. When you're buying from a shop, there are qualified salespeople to help you. But when you buy from an individual, you're on your own when it comes to the condition of the bike, sizing, and fit.

Your first step in buying a used bike is pretty simple: ask the owner why he or she is selling it. From your point of view as the buyer, the best reasons are that the owner simply doesn't find the time to ride or doesn't enjoy mountain biking (hard to believe), or any other reason that results in a bike that was ridden only on Sundays by a little old lady from Pasadena.

It's really the same as buying a used car. You want to avoid buying a bike that has been beaten and abused. The difference is that bikes don't have factory-installed odometers, and I doubt if you'll find a mountain biker who has a full set of service records. So you need to ask the right questions. Of course, it's not likely that someone will tell you the bike has had the tar beat out of it. It's up to you to diagnose the health of the bike.

Start by doing the Quick Check (see pages 76–78). If you find just a few things that need adjusting, it's no big deal. But if almost everything is out of whack it can give you an idea of how well the bike was maintained (or not maintained). Suppose when you check the

A good deal is not always what it seems.

headset, you find it has an inch of play in it and it knocks so much it sounds like someone's at the door. You ask the owner, "How long has the headset been like this?" He says, "Huh? Like what?" You should think twice about buying this bike.

Here are a few items you should take into account when buying a used bike. You're looking for symptoms of possible problems. Consider whether the things you need to replace will end up costing more than the bike is worth in the first place:

1. Inspect the rims for excessive wear. If the sidewalls are cupped significantly (worn to the point of being concave instead of flat), the bike has been around the block a few times and the rims should be replaced.

2. Look at the grips. A bike with a lot of miles on it will have grips that are noticeably worn.

3. Take a look at the tires. Look for worn tread and cuts in the rubber. Some soft-compound tires wear very quickly, so take this into account. If all the little nubbies are still on the tire, then you know that either the tires were replaced or the bike has not been ridden very much.

4. Check out the seat. A seat will, over time, have a torn and abraded cover. Bent rails can also be a sign of lots of hard riding.

5. Slide the seat post all the way down into the seat tube. A bent seat post is a sign of abusive riding and will not lower all the way into the seat tube.

These are all cumulative problems that occur with ordinary use. Take a notebook along and make notes about what you find. If the bike has been well maintained and the price is right, you may decide that a little wear is OK. On the other hand, if there are two pages of problems, you may want to continue your search.

If the bike has passed your inspection but you still have some doubts, ask the owner if you can take the bike to a shop to have it checked out for more inconspicuous problems. Of course, I wouldn't let someone walk away with my bike without some kind of deposit, so expect to leave a check for the purchase price of the bike, and agree that you will buy the bike if no problems are found. Postdate the check so the sale can be voided if there are major problems discovered at the shop. For peace of mind, the owner may feel better about this arrangement if he or she goes with you to the shop, or if he or she takes the bike personally. Ask the shop for a written estimate to get the bike up to par and expect to pay something for the mechanic's time. Use this estimate to bargain with the owner on price.

A bike's value depreciates over time, just like a car's. Unfortunately, there's no little blue book of used bike prices. Generally speaking, a one-year-old bike in good condition is worth 30 percent less than it was new. A two-year-old bike, 50 percent less. That's if the bike is in good shape except for ordinary wear and tear. Deduct major expenses, like replacing a headset or bottom bracket or replacing seals in the suspension fork, from this figure. Ask the owner how much the bike cost new, and what accessories were added. If the bike is being sold with a pump and tool kit, extra tires, and spare parts, you should expect to pay a little more.

ACCESSORIES

If you've always had a glamorous picture of mountain biking accessories, what you are about to read may disappoint you.

When you actually hit the trail, Day-Glo tights, talking odometers, and hydraulic riding shoes are not—believe it or not—necessities. In fact, I've always believed that the less you carry, the better you ride. Aside from the fact that attachments can burden you, a ton of accessories just adds a barrier between you and your bike. For me, anyway, less is more when it comes to biking.

For some people, accessories take on another dimension. Riding props become distractions, a quick fix for big problems, or a crutch. At that point, you need to ask yourself: What do I really need, as opposed to what I think I need? Yes, better tires can help your riding—but how much of the ride is about the tires and how much is about you? What part of the process are you not taking advantage of so that you think you need new tires? Are you externalizing, when in fact you might need simply to focus on riding better and think a little bit more about what you're doing?

There's no quick fix. Accessories are facilitators; they offer assistance, but they can't make up for a lack of know-how. I've seen guys at Mount Snow on $3,000 bikes made of recycled space shuttles, with the bike pump that hides in the seat post, wearing the titanium underwear—and they're the ones who have no clue what to do if they get a flat on the trail.

Don't be a slave to fashion or to anyone's dictates. Just because someone tells you you need something, don't automatically head to the bike store and buy it. Understand what you need and why before you spend a dime. Everyone recommends an Allen wrench set, and most new riders run out and buy one. But if you don't know how to use it, it's irrelevant. People get outfitted with CO_2 cartridges, tools, patch kits—and if anything happens on the trail, they have no clue what to do. Learn, understand, and practice.

Of course, I've also seen the other extreme—guys in baggy shorts and tie-dyed T-shirts riding bikes with their bare feet in Teva sandals, no helmet, no patch kit. No good. Somewhere in the middle is a place where you've thought about everything you need, whether each item functions as you intend it should, and whether or not you need it. It's up to you, for example, what to put in your saddlebag. You could carry a bowling ball if you had room enough, but do you really want to? Think of your gear as luggage. And follow that tried-and-true rule of packing: put in everything you think you need, then take half of it out. Don't depend on accessories or make them a crutch. Too many riders do, and it becomes a hard habit to break.

Let the buyer beware: some totally ridiculous accessories have also hit bike stores in the last couple of years. Two in particular come to mind for sheer inanity. Sedis, a French company, introduced a gas-powered mountain bike motor that defeats the purpose of biking. You can also buy a pump from an American company that hooks up to your bike chain and pumps while you pedal. Pretty clever, but its bulk and weight make it completely impractical.

But at the very least, you'll need to invest in a basic tool kit as outlined in chapter 4, plus protective eyewear and a Snell- or ANSI-approved helmet. Each item serves a particular purpose, helping to make riding safer and more comfortable. Here's what to look for in each.

HELMETS

There are two different rating systems for helmets: Snell and ANSI. Both organizations test helmets by dropping pointy objects from great heights onto the helmets and observing the results. Their endorsements mean a helmet meets a standard of protection. The standards are strict and universal, so virtually every helmet you'll see should carry a sticker from either group. I wouldn't make anyone endure another helmet lecture, but it can't be stressed enough. I know several people who would be dead if they hadn't been wearing helmets when they crashed. But a helmet shouldn't lull you into complacency, just as air bags and seat belts shouldn't in a car. It protects you in certain specific situations. It doesn't grant you carte blanche to ride wildly or recklessly. If you fly over the handlebars and land on your face, a helmet won't help you. It's minimal protection. Use common sense to know when you're doing something you shouldn't. Keep injuries from happening in the first place—that's your best protection.

Pay attention to fit, ventilation, and weight to make sure you buy a helmet that suits you. The way a helmet fits is extremely important. Make sure your helmet sits level on your head,

protecting your forehead as well as the top of your head. We've all seen riders with their helmets tipped toward the back of their heads. The strap dangles loosely below the chin and the helmet looks like it could slip off the back of the head. This is dangerous. Think about it. What's the most likely point of impact if you were to fall off your bike and hit your head? That's right, your face. When the helmet is hanging off the back of your head it won't do anything to protect you in a face plant. Keep the helmet forward with the chin strap adjusted snugly. Ask a qualified salesperson to help choose a helmet that has the right fit for you (another good reason not to buy from a catalog).

At a race at Mount Snow recently, one kid had cut the arms and legs from a doll, glued them to the sides of a helmet, and stuck the doll's head on top—with an orange mohawk. No one said mountain bikers were subtle.

PROTECTIVE EYEWEAR

Small-lens sunglasses may look cool, but you won't think so when your eyes are dripping with tears from a whipping wind. Instead, you'll want wraparound sunglasses for good peripheral vision. You must wear shatterproof lenses, which you'll find in plastic and polycarbonate. For obvious reasons, you should leave the glass lenses at home.

It's best to carry interchangeable dark, orange, and clear lenses to get the optimal protection in any light level. Some people get sunglasses only, but you can't wear those when the sun sets. You'll want to keep your eyewear on some kind of leash or retention strap, so that when you hit that big bump they don't fly into the mud and disappear. And once again, you don't need to spend $140 on glasses, even though there are frames that expensive on the market. I've seen many frames that look and fit fine for much less.

If you must wear glasses full time, your frames can function as your eye protection. Try to get frames that take clip-on sunglasses. Goggles on top of your glasses might be overkill—you'll look like a giant bug on a mountain bike.

Make sure that whatever kind of glasses you get offer some degree of UV light protection. Ultraviolet radiation is the suspected cause of cataracts, a clouding of the cornea commonly seen in older people. The more UV light you're exposed to over your lifetime, the more likely you are to get cataracts. It's important for those who spend a lot of time outdoors, especially at high altitudes (UV radiation is more intense at high elevations), to protect their eyes.

SHOES

Most major athletic shoe manufacturers now make biking shoes, distinguished by their stiff soles. Remember what we said about weight versus strength in chapter 2? It's just as important for your shoes to be strong and light as it is any other part of your bike. A stiff sole means efficient power transfer from your foot to the drive train.

By now, you've probably surmised that I'm an organic kind of guy. But when it comes to mountain biking shoes, I make an exception. Nothing beats synthetic materials. They don't

stretch or give a lot. For the same reason you want a stiff sole you also should have shoes that fit snugly. Your foot will move around in a shoe that's too big, resulting in poor power transfer to the drive train. Leather can start snug, but it will end up very loose from moisture or just regular wear. One brand of shoe that I used to wear was natural leather; I went through three sizes, going down in size each time, before I found one that worked, because the leather stretched so much. You also want well-ventilated mesh in the upper, or your feet will sweat profusely.

Virtually every mountain bike shoe is now also SPD (Shimano Pedaling Dynamics, or Shimano's brand of clipless pedals). Most other brands of clipless pedals have used Shimano's cleat pattern in order to be compatible with most shoes—meaning there's a cutout on the sole where you can install cleats. The best also have Velcro straps as well as laces instead of either-or; Velcro wears out over time and eventually snaps, so you want laces, too. But straps are great for snugging up.

You'll find shoes at different price levels. Once again, it's the old strength-weight equation. Lighter, stiffer shoes are more expensive; softer, heavier shoes cost less. Some riders might prefer low-end shoes. They're softer, more comfortable, cheaper, and better for walking when you're not riding. Just because they're expensive, serious racing shoes aren't for everyone. I've had to talk people out of buying racing shoes because I knew they'd be miserable.

GLOVES

Gloves are an important and often overlooked accessory. A padded glove can prevent carpal tunnel syndrome, an annoying nerve disorder that's a result of constant gripping. You've probably heard about carpal tunnel syndrome; it happens when the nerves in your hand are chronically compressed, producing numbness and tingling in the fingers. Windsurfers, tennis players, and people who spend a lot of time in front of a computer are also prone to suffer from it.

Choose a glove that's a little snug to allow for stretching. You'll want plenty of ventilation and a patch of terry cloth on the back, for wiping the sweat out of your eyes. I prefer an unpadded glove with three-quarter fingers, that is, ones that leave about an inch of your fingertip exposed. Unpadded gloves give you more of a connection to your handlebars, and I like to be able to feel every bit of information coming to me through my bike. A padded glove muddies the feeling of connectedness to the trail, but giving it up is a sacrifice when it comes to comfort.

CLOTHING

Padded shorts are a must for anyone considering putting in time on a bike. Shorts come in the tight Lycra variety and in a baggy snowboarder kind of look. Either way, get padded shorts. If you want to spare the world the sight of your body in Lycra, wear baggy gym shorts over a pair of padded Lycra shorts. Women should look for shorts that are designed for the female body. Most bike clothing manufactur-

ers make women's shorts, but not all shops carry them. If you have trouble finding anatomically correct shorts try looking in a bike mail-order catalog.

Even with padded shorts, your butt will get sore at first, but the pad should make the pain more bearable. Here I go sounding like your mother again, but make sure you wear a clean pair of shorts each time you ride. A pad that's been previously worn is a breeding ground for bacteria. Any broken skin will become infected and you could end up with big boils on your behind—nice, huh?

If you're looking for tights to wear in cooler weather, I suggest getting unpadded tights. That way, you can wear padded shorts underneath the tights, and when it warms up, shed the tights.

Jerseys can keep you cool and dry in warm weather, and the pockets in the back make carrying a banana and a spare tube convenient, but they don't seem to have caught on with the mountain biking crowd. I suspect it's largely because of cost; a jersey can cost upward of $65. Not only that, but mountain biking is just as tough on clothing as it is on bikes. More than once, I can remember ripping a brand new pair of Lycra shorts to shreds on briars— that's $35 down the drain. I suspect most mountain bikers would rather tear up a $14 T-shirt than a $65 jersey.

If you decide that a jersey is for you, make your choice based on price, fit, and style. A jersey shouldn't be too tight; you'll want air to circulate between your body and the material, allowing perspiration to evaporate. Windbreakers (also called shells) should also have plenty of room in them so you can dress in layers when it's chilly. Choose a shell made from a breathable fabric that has vents built in to help ventilate your body and keep you dry while you ride. Other things to look for in a shell are zippered pockets so you don't lose your map and reflective material for riding at dusk or in the dark.

BAGS AND RACKS

Now that you've got all this stuff you need to be able to put it somewhere. There are any number of saddlebags, handlebar bags, and packs that go on your back, on a rack, or around your waist. It's a difficult decision; there's a huge number of products to choose from.

If you plan to do most of your riding on the trail, I recommend carrying your gear using a combination of saddlebag and waist pack. A saddlebag hangs under, and attaches to, the rails of your seat. Saddlebags come in various sizes and some even zip open to expand for longer trips. I carry all my tools in a saddlebag, tucked out of the way where it can't catch on branches. When I'm done with my ride I can leave it on my bike, ready for the next ride. Choose a saddlebag that attaches with sturdy Velcro straps. Some bags have fancy nylon clips that allow you to pop the bag on and off without fumbling with straps. The only problem is that the nylon is very brittle and can break easily when subjected to the pounding and vibration of the trail.

I carry the rest of my gear—extra clothes, food, maps, and so on—in a waist pack. I like this best because its weight is distributed on my body with neutral effect. A backpack distributes its weight on your neck, shoulders, and back. While that's okay for hiking—when your body is upright—it won't work on a bike, when you tend to have a more horizontal upper body. You'll develop a sore neck from the weight of the pack.

Another thing I don't recommend for trail riding is a rear rack. For years I guided students carrying most of my gear in a pack mounted on a rear rack. Eventually I figured out that the weight of the rack and all that gear was making my bike top-heavy. It handled poorly in tight single track and in any slow situation requiring balance.

A waist pack, however, is situated at your center of gravity. It moves with your body, not with your bike, so that bike handling is not affected. Notice I'm talking about a waist pack and not a fanny pack. Waist packs, also known as lumbar packs, ride higher than a fanny pack and with proper strap adjustment will not droop down and hang off your butt the way a fanny pack will.

Forget about panniers. They are strictly for touring bikes and will not do well on the trail. If you're planning on doing some mountain bike camping, where you ride roads from camp to camp, and then use the camp as a base to make day trips, panniers make sense; otherwise leave them at home.

UPGRADING YOUR BIKE

Once you've gotten your bike, tools, and clothes, and you still have money to spend, you can consider upgrading your bike. I've never been one to go crazy getting new doodads or bells and whistles for my bike. My theory is, if it's not broke, use it!

Nowadays you see guys with purple titanium water bottle cages and hubs that look like they came from Mars. But unless you've got money to burn, or your friends won't talk to you anymore without the latest accessory du jour, my advice is to hang on to your money. Titanium is very light stuff. The problem is that it's also extremely expensive, and the weight you save isn't all that great. We're talking a few grams, max. If you're a pro racer, you need to save every gram you can. If you're someone like me, you could probably save more weight just by not eating any Ben and Jerry's Wavy Gravy ice cream for a week.

A couple of upgrades, however, can improve your riding and are worth every penny:

Bar Ends. I don't know how I ever rode without bar ends. Along with clipless pedals, bar ends were responsible for taking my riding to a new level. Also called climbing bars, bar ends extend your reach, helping you shift your weight forward in the climb. And because of the additional hand positions, fatigue is greatly reduced. In my mind bar ends should be standard equipment on all mountain bikes.

Choose a pair of bar ends that fits into your hand comfortably. Some are designed with a weld to make them curve, others are bent. It's really a matter of personal preference which you choose. Avoid steel or chrome-moly models—they weigh more than they need to. Aluminum is strong and very light and will set you back $45 to $60.

Clipless Pedals. Because of their high cost, only high-end bikes come from the factory with clipless pedals. But I strongly recommend springing for a pair as soon as you can afford to. Clipless pedals will give you more power in your pedal stroke, and more stability in the single track.

There are many different systems out there, but I recommend a spring-loaded mechanical system. They're heavier than other systems that use urethane bumpers and other mechanisms, but are the most reliable. One thing you want to avoid is not releasing from your pedals when you need to, or pre-releasing in a rocky downhill.

At first, clips will feel like you can't get out when you want to; set the spring tension as loose as possible so you can get out easily, but not so loose that you come out when you don't want to. You need to learn to twist to get out of the pedal instead of pulling your foot back, as you do with clips and straps. Clipless pedals will set you back anywhere from $150 to $300.

Suspension Fork. I usually don't recommend retrofitting a rigid-frame bike with a suspension fork. This is because if the bike was not designed for suspension, the addition of a suspension fork will change the frame geometry. When you add a suspension fork to a rigid-frame bike it raises the front of the bike, usually about 1 inch. The result is a bike with shallower head tube and seat tube angles and very different handling characteristics.

But over the last couple of years a few manufacturers have been changing the design of their rigid-frame bikes so that the addition of a suspension fork does not alter the geometry. If you're shopping for a new bike and you're not ready to spring for a suspended model, ask if the bike has suspension-corrected geometry. If it does, then sometime down the road, after you win the lottery, you can add a fork without adversely affecting the handling of the bike. Choose a fork based on the type of riding you'll be doing. A suspension fork will cost you anywhere from $200 to $600.

■ ■ ■

Anyone who tells you that decent accessories must cost a fortune is lying. It isn't always necessary to have the best of everything. Whenever I've bought glasses, a derailleur, or tools, I've always tried to find the cheapest stuff that does what I need it to do. Mountain biking is so hard on equipment, and most parts and accessories take such serious abuse, that I'd rather break something that cost $20 instead of $80. Yes, it feels wonderful to own the latest, jazziest accessories. But you're going to beat the hell out of them, so why spend all that money? Yes, cheap parts wear out faster, but consider this: I've broken most derailleurs long before I've ever had the chance to wear them out.

If you have trouble deciding what to buy and for how much, consult your bike store. Though bike stores make most of their money off accessories, the ones I've dealt with have been remarkably honest and helpful. Unfortunately, small and even medium dealers can't compete with catalog merchants. Bicycle catalogs will sometimes list items for just $2 or $3

more than we pay for them wholesale at Mount Snow. So don't expect bike shops to match the prices you rattle off from catalogs—in fact, you'll probably set off the store owner by trying!

Think of your shop as a community resource center, and support it. Of course, you can look up whatever you need in one of the many bike-supply catalogs that keep springing up as biking gets hotter. But keep in mind that bike shops are enthusiastic supporters of the sport and deserve your support in return. You can save money by shopping mail order; for big-ticket items, in fact, you should think of doing it. But once you become a regular customer at a good bike shop, the level of service has tangible value.

People would walk into the Mount Snow store, see something like a rear derailleur or suspension fork, and insist they could find it for some crazy price through a catalog. I say fine, do it—but see if they have it in stock, wait four to six weeks, then when you have a problem with it, see if someone from the catalog company will take it apart to see what's wrong, then call the manufacturer to help you. If you're buying a pair of gloves or shoes, it's one thing. But for anything that involves maintenance or advice, think twice.

Like many neighborhood shops threatened by superstores, small bike stores are an endangered species. As bike chain stores get bigger, they're crowding out the smaller ones. Not every bike shop fits my Norman Rockwell characterization, but most are interested in their customers and are willing to answer questions and offer all-around help. It's important for the stores themselves to develop a biking community and make themselves the hub (no pun intended), so many sponsor evening rides and local races.

One last word about biking accoutrements. I'm not a fashion critic, but I've always felt that people who dress like racers to ride in the woods look kind of silly. I'm still of the T-shirt variety of rider, though I do wear Lycra shorts. Mountain bikers are so out there anyway, there's nothing you could do fashionwise to shock them.

6

......

THE MOUNTAIN BIKE WAY
TO HEALTH AND FITNESS

Training, Conditioning, and Nutrition

You've heard it from the surgeon general, your old gym teacher, and now from me: regular exercise prolongs life and, more important, enhances the quality of life. Being fit helps you handle daily challenges with vitality. It instills confidence and a sense of accomplishment, and fosters a healthy can-do attitude in all aspects of your life. You can gain all of the above from mountain biking. And best of all, because it's so much fun, you won't even notice how hard you're working.

When it's under stress, the human body adapts by getting stronger. When you exercise vigorously on a regular basis, your body begins recognizing the change and learns to prepare itself for steady exertion. As a result, the heart becomes stronger and more efficient, arteries enlarge to accommodate increased blood flow, lungs increase their capacity to absorb oxygen from the air, and muscles involved in the workout become stronger.

My own training schedule consists of a combination of strength and endurance exercises. Mountain biking is much more body-active than road riding and requires upper-body strength, especially on technical terrain. You'll find your riding improves much more rapidly if you expand your routine to include strength training along with cardiovascular training.

In fairness, I should tell you I'm not an exercise physiologist. But I have spent years educating myself on how exercise affects the body—and how to make the most of my riding. The information in this chapter is intended to help you achieve a better level of fitness. It's in no way meant as a complete or scientific essay on the subject. Take the time to educate yourself to gain a more complete knowledge of exercise physiology. And, of course, always seek the advice of your physician when embarking on an exercise program.

You'll know you're truly fit when you're strong in each of the following areas:

1. **Aerobic capacity:** The ability of the heart and lungs to deliver oxygen to the muscles and vital organs.
2. **Strength:** The capacity of your muscles to exert force on an object.
3. **Endurance:** The ability to sustain physical effort over a period of time.
4. **Flexibility:** The ability of the joints and muscles to move over a full range of motion.
5. **Health:** The ability of the body to repair itself and mitigate stresses put upon it.

To increase your level of fitness, train regularly and follow proven exercise physiology principles.

AEROBIC FITNESS

Aerobic means "with air"; aerobic exercise is physical activity powered by the oxygen captured by the lungs and distributed to the muscles and vital organs via the heart and blood vessels. The goal of aerobic training is to increase the amount of oxygen your body is able to absorb and deliver to your muscles at a faster rate. This increased capacity allows you to ride harder and longer.

Your body reacts to the increased demands of exercise by breathing faster to absorb more oxygen and upping your heartbeat. That way, it can deliver more oxygen to your muscles more quickly so you can sustain this new level of activity.

Muscles are powered by two methods: by oxygen delivered through the bloodstream (aerobic), and by sugars (glycogen) stored in the muscles and liver (anaerobic). The aerobic method of powering your muscles is the most effective and efficient, but it has its limitations. Depending on your level of fitness, there's a point when your cardiovascular system (heart, lungs, and vessels that circulate blood) cannot supply enough oxygen to meet the demands of very strenuous exercise. This is called the anaerobic threshold—the point at which your body begins to use stored sugars to power the muscles. High-intensity, short-duration activities, like sprinting up a steep hill, tend to be anaerobic in nature, while moderate-intensity, long-term activities tend to be aerobic.

Learn to recognize when you've reached the threshold. You'll know you're there when you're gasping for air as you hit that steep hill. The gorp you ate for lunch is in imminent danger of reappearing. If you keep pushing hard at the threshold, you'll reach a point where everything shuts down and you feel like you can't continue. If you pull back and slow down, however, you'll drop back below the anaerobic threshold and probably continue up the hill, albeit at a slower pace.

Like any other strenuous activity, mountain biking is a combination of aerobic and anaerobic exercise. Steadily increasing your aerobic capacity will also help you raise the anaerobic threshold—and let you tackle big hills without "going anaerobic."

HEART RATE

Three numbers are important in assessing your aerobic fitness. First is your *resting heart rate,* the beats per minute your heart needs to

maintain basic body functions at rest. Second, your *maximum heart rate* is the highest rate you're physiologically able to achieve. Finally, your *training* (or *target*) *rate* is the rate at which you derive the maximum benefit—an improvement in performance—from your exercise. Your training rate is expressed as a percentage of your maximum rate.

To check your heart rate press gently on one side of your neck just to the side of your windpipe with the tips of your index and middle fingers. Feel your pulse at the carotid artery. Count the beats for fifteen seconds and multiply by four. This is your heart rate. If you want to spend some money, an electronic heart monitor can be very helpful for keeping track of your heart's activity during exercise. Heart monitors feature digital displays of your heart rate at any given moment to provide instant feedback while on the trail and can help to maximize the effectiveness of your training.

RESTING RATE

Your resting rate is the rate at which your heart beats when you're sitting around watching *One Life to Live.* It's a good indicator of your overall fitness. Check your resting rate

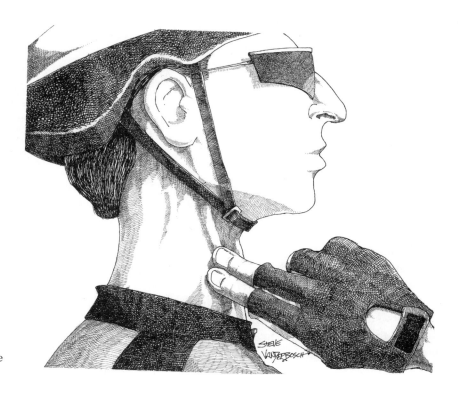

Find your pulse at the carotid artery.

first thing in the morning when you get out of bed, before you've had your coffee. An untrained individual's heart rate will be relatively high, 70 to 80 beats per minute (bpm), while a fit person's resting rate will be as low as 50 or even 45 bpm. When an unfit individual is at rest the heart must work harder at maintaining body functions because his or her capacity (the highest possible level of exertion) is lower. Resting represents a more significant proportion of the person's overall capacity than in a fit person.

Sally is fit enough to handle only the simplest tasks of day-to-day life—walking, carrying groceries, climbing stairs. For Sally, sitting on a couch at rest represents a larger percentage of her capacity; her heart rate is around 80 bpm at rest. Sarah, on the other hand, is an accomplished mountain biker. For her, exertion means riding a mountain bike for three hours at 10,000 feet. When she lounges around on the couch, her body has to work much less hard to maintain body functions. Sarah's resting rate is 50 beats per minute.

Sarah's heart has become larger and stronger by responding to the demands strenuous training has put upon it. The heart has become larger because her muscles need lots of oxygen-rich blood to make them go. Her lungs have become more efficient as well, taking in a larger volume of air to supply essential oxygen. The rate at which the cardiovascular system can deliver oxygen is called *oxygen uptake*.

The heart is a muscle, and like any other muscle its strength and performance can be improved through exercise. There are specific guidelines that have been developed to maximize the benefits of exercise.

MAXIMUM AND TARGET HEART RATES

Your target heart rate is the rate at which your body derives the most benefit during exercise. The ideal target range is 60 to 85 percent of your maximum heart rate. To significantly improve your aerobic capacity, you must train within your target rate for at least thirty minutes during your ride. Estimate your maximum heart rate using the following formula: 220 minus your age. If you are twenty-two years old, your maximum heart rate is estimated to be 198 (220 – 22); if you are forty-five, it would be about 175 (220 – 45).

Bear in mind that these are estimates only. You can pinpoint your maximum rate more accurately by taking a treadmill stress test, which involves a progressively tougher jog on a treadmill. Your oxygen uptake and your heart's performance are monitored electronically throughout the test, which is the same exam given to heart patients and professional athletes—and the best way to get a really accurate reading of your overall fitness. Consult your physician or see a sports medicine specialist to get a stress test.

According to the formula, I should have a maximum heart rate of 180, or 220 minus 40. My training rate, 80 percent of that, would be 144. Problem is, I know my maximum rate is really around 200. I clocked it at 206 with a heart monitor this past summer while riding to the summit of Mount Snow. That means that, using 206 as my maximum, my training rate is really 165—a significant difference. If I trained at 144 bpm, I'd cheat myself out of the maximum benefit from training.

The formula to estimate maximum heart

rate is probably a good starting point for anyone just getting into physical training. But if you've already got years of exercise under your belt, it may be worthwhile to get a more accurate determination of maximum rate using the stress test.

How Do I Do It?

Why, you ask yourself, must I go through all this trouble? Why can't I just ride and have fun?

You *can* have fun while you train, but you won't if you think training and fun are mutually exclusive. All it takes is monitoring your heart rate while you ride and making sure that at least a portion of your ride produces heart rates in the training range.

The minimum time you should spend training is thirty minutes, three times a week. This means thirty minutes of sustained heart rate within your training range. It's recommended that beginning athletes train at 60 to 70 percent of their maximum heart rate. Experienced athletes may train as high as 90 percent of their maximum. If you're thirty-four years old and training at 70 percent, your target heart rate is 130. You should stretch thoroughly, then spend five to ten minutes warming up at 50 to 60 percent of your maximum. After your warmup, pick up the pace and raise your rate to your training level. Keep it there, without a break, for a minimum of thirty minutes, then cool down for ten to fifteen minutes before you stop and stretch again. The stretching and the warmup and cooldown are intended to prevent injury and lessen the shock of sudden stress to your muscles and joints.

On longer rides, monitor your rate during a specific portion of the ride. It doesn't matter when in the ride it is. I like to incorporate a hill climb into this portion of my ride, but if you don't have long climbs it could be a section of fire road, pavement, or single track. Once you've finished the training portion of your ride, relax and enjoy the rest of your ride.

Trail riding often doesn't raise your heart rate to training levels, especially in the flatlands. If the terrain is technical, you just can't move fast enough to keep your heart in the training rate, uninterrupted, for thirty to forty minutes. The best way to raise your heart rate is by climbing. Be thankful for any big hills in your area. There are lots of people out there who would kill to have steep terrain. If you have hills, ride them!

To find out if your heart is getting the workout it needs, take a ride on your favorite trail. Give it all you've got and see if you can get your heart rate into the training range. If you can't, then follow this heretical advice, and don't tell anyone I'm the one who told you to do it . . .

Ride your mountain bike on the road!

Yes, it sounds like it contradicts everything I stand for. But it improves your mountain biking. What you need is more resistance to push against, more work to get that heart pumping. Riding those big fat knobbies on the pavement, or even on a dirt road, will give you plenty to work with. Ride your bike as fast as you can on the road and see how it works; if you have to, let some air out of your tires. If there's a wind, ride right into it; it'll feel like hell when you're doing it, but like banging your head against a wall, it feels great when you stop! After your warmup, ride the road for thirty to forty minutes—enough to get the training benefit you need. Then go have fun on the trail. The idea is to get that heart rate up. *Doing that regularly will improve your speed and endurance while trail riding.*

STRENGTH TRAINING

Your muscles also respond to stress by getting stronger. When you work your muscles hard they get sore. Sore muscles are actually torn on a microscopic level. When the body repairs torn muscle cells, it anticipates future stresses by adding muscle tissue. This makes your muscles bigger, firmer, and stronger.

Mountain biking by itself will not exercise your muscles adequately to give you a complete strength training session. Cycling uses primarily the quadriceps (the front of the upper leg) of your legs. The hamstring muscles (the back of your upper leg) are used to a much lesser degree, which can cause an imbalance in the relative strength of these two opposing muscle groups. Studies show that such an imbalance can contribute to knee injuries, since the quadriceps and hamstring muscles are to a large extent responsible for the stability of the knee joint. An imbalance creates unequal forces on the knee and can injure ligaments and tendons, or aggravate previous injuries. By including hamstring exercises in a weight-training routine you can greatly reduce your risk of knee injury.

Include weight training in your routine at least twice a week during your riding season and four times a week off season. You don't need to go crazy—we're not trying to become the next Arnold. Find a gym with an informed, helpful staff and ask for help designing a routine. Use free weights, machines, whatever feels comfortable and convenient. A weight-training routine should include all the major muscle groups and shouldn't take more than 1½ hours in the gym per session.

You may also consider home gym equipment. While this is more convenient, and more economical over the long term, I prefer the variety of equipment in gyms.

Your training should stay focused, progressive, and goal oriented. When you go to the gym, you should know your routine. Walk into the weight room and get right to work. Don't gab with friends, and whatever you do once you warm up, don't let yourself cool down until you're done. Start out with a minimum amount of weight and work your way up gradually. Strength training exercises are usually organized in units of "reps" and "sets." A rep, or repetition, is one complete execution of the particular exercise. A set is a grouping of reps. I've had the best results with three sets of eight reps on any particular exercise.

To progress with any training routine, you need clear goals, both long- and short-term, and a plan on how to achieve them. At the gym, I choose a weight that I can handle for eight reps and three sets. The last couple of reps in the last set should be difficult. When you can easily complete three full sets of eight reps, then it's time to increase the weight. Increase by the smallest increment possible and continue the process. At first you'll improve by leaps and bounds, but after a while you'll slow down and may even reach a plateau, where you find it difficult to increase your weights.

When lifting, whether it's with free weights or a machine, it's important to keep a few things in mind:

- Control the weight. Move the weight slowly and deliberately. It's possible to handle more weight when you move it quickly and explosively, but you won't derive as much benefit from the exercise and you'll be more likely to injure yourself.

- Move the weight through a full range of motion. Maximum benefit from a movement can be obtained only when the joints and muscles are flexed and extended through their full range of motion.

- Don't exercise the same muscle groups on consecutive days. Muscles need at least a full day's rest before being stressed again. This step is key in allowing muscle tissue to adapt to exercise and become stronger. Separate your training into two routines, upper body and lower body. For example, work out your upper body on Mondays and Thursdays (or any other nonconsecutive days that work for you) off season and on Mondays only during the riding season. Work out your lower body on Tuesdays and Fridays off season, and Fridays only during the season.

- Start each exercise with a warmup set. Before you use a heavier weight, warm up for one set with a weight you can handle easily for twelve to fifteen reps. This will ensure your muscles are ready to handle the heavier weights of subsequent sets, and will serve as additional injury prevention.

- Focus on your weak points. If you have exceptionally strong quads but relatively weak calves, put your calf exercises early in your routine, when you have the most energy. Your quads are strong, so they don't need extra attention, but if you ignore or underexercise your calves they'll never get stronger. (Those aren't calves, they're steers!) By devoting your energy to areas that aren't as strong as others you can develop a more well-rounded fitness.

Include all major muscle groups in your routine, and be sure to include a warmup followed by a thorough stretching before lifting. A hundred jumping jacks or five to ten minutes on a stationary bicycle, treadmill, or stair-climbing machine to warm up will elevate your heart rate and increase the blood flow to your muscles. The increased blood flow will help your muscles perform better and can help to prevent injuries, while an elevated heart rate will prepare you for the exertion of your workout.

You will experience muscle soreness at first; it's part of the package and entirely normal. Be patient. It comes with the early phase of strength training and it, too, shall pass. Avoid hot tubs and Jacuzzis during this period, as heat will aggravate the soreness. What is not normal is joint pain. If you experience pain in any joint after lifting, stop the exercise for a while and see a doctor before resuming your workout.

To get you started, I've brought together a sampling of some free-weight exercises. There are literally hundreds of different strength-training exercises for machines and free weights. The exercises included here are by no means intended to be the only exercises for these muscle groups. But if you do one of each, or a close alternative, you'll get a complete workout of all major muscle groups. Ask the staff at your gym or read a strength-training book or magazine to develop a routine to meet your specific needs.

UPPER BODY

The muscles of the upper body (chest, back, arms) are used in mountain biking to maneuver the bike through rough terrain, jump obstacles, and in cornering. Since these are not the primary muscles involved in the propulsion of the bike, the muscles of the upper body do not receive regular training while riding. For this reason it's as important (if not more) to strengthen the muscles of the upper body as it is to train the legs.

Chest: Push-ups, Bench Presses

Push-ups are a great way to increase the strength in your chest without any equipment. Place your hands directly under your shoulders, and with your feet together push your entire body off the floor until your arms are almost fully extended. Keep your neck, back, and legs in as straight a line as possible. Bring your body back to the floor slowly, controlling the descent. Do as many as you can up to around fifty, then rest for thirty to sixty seconds and repeat. If you're having trouble getting your entire body off the floor, do your push-ups from the knees up only. Instead of pivoting off the floor at your feet, leave your lower legs flat on the floor and pivot at the knees. If you'd like to increase the difficulty of push-ups, move your hands to the outside of your shoulders. Push-ups also make a great warmup exercise. When done as a warmup for strength training, do two sets of twenty push-ups.

Bench presses are a great way to increase upper-body strength. Not only do bench presses increase strength in your chest muscles, they also train, to a lesser degree, your back, triceps (the muscles on the back of your upper arm), forearms, and hands—all important muscles in mountain biking.

Lay flat on your back on a bench with a pressing rack. Never do bench presses without someone standing at your head to "spot" you. A spotter can help you with the weight if you tire midway through a repetition.

Start with a very low weight (20 to 25 percent of your body weight) for the first set, and have the spotter help you lower the weight to your chest. Be sure to account for the weight of the bar when choosing which plates to use. The bar should be resting on your chest at about the nipple line. Push the bar up, away from your chest, in a straight line, 90 degrees to your body. Push until your arms are nearly locked out, then return the weight to your chest slowly, under control. Repeat twelve times. Increase the weight for the next two sets. Choose a weight that you can handle comfortably for eight to ten reps, but the last rep of the last set should be difficult to complete. Your ultimate goal (it could take years) should be to be able to bench your body weight.

Bench press

Arms: Biceps Curls, Triceps Extensions, Wrist Curls

Strong arm muscles are especially important in high-speed rough terrain, when a strong grip and the ability to hang on can mean the difference between dumping it and making it.

Biceps curls train the biceps muscles of your upper arms (the muscles at the front of your upper arm). There are special "curl" bars that are curved in such a way as to keep your wrists at an ergonomically correct angle to prevent wrist injuries.

Again, choose a light weight for your first set, about 10 percent of your body weight. Stand with your feet shoulder-width apart and your back straight. With the bar at arm's length and your palms facing away from you, lift the weight by moving your hands and lower arms in an arc, up and toward your chest. Your elbows should stay tucked in at your sides and your upper arms should not move at all during the movement. Repeat twelve times and increase the weight for the following two sets, executed as explained in the section on bench pressing.

Biceps curl

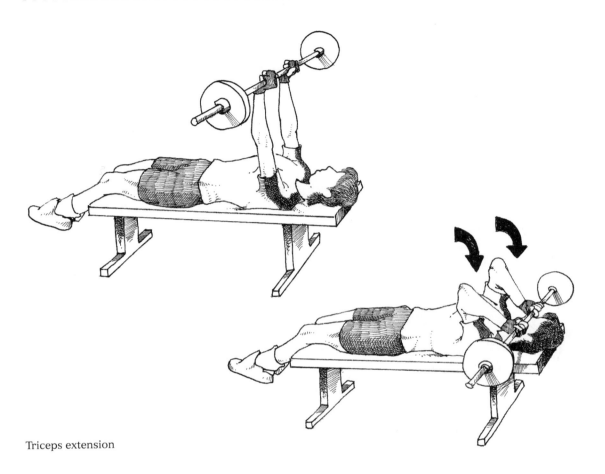

Triceps extension

Triceps extensions train the triceps muscles of your upper arm. Strong triceps muscles are especially useful during any activity that requires a strong grip. (Anything come to mind?)

Have someone spot for you, and using a curl bar without any weight on it, lie on a bench, on your back with your feet flat on the floor. Use a bench without a bar rack. Extend your arms overhead with your palms facing away from you and have your spotter hand you the bar. Lower the bar slowly toward your forehead in

a semicircle without moving your upper arms. Return to the extended position and repeat eight to twelve times. Be sure your spotter is ready to take control of the weight if you have any trouble. An empty bar should be plenty of weight at first. If even that is too much, try using dumbbells (around five pounds) instead of a bar. Perform the exercise in the same way, but only one arm at a time. Add weight slowly with this exercise, in increments of five pounds or less.

Wrist curls increase the strength of the forearms and hands, also very important during any gripping activity.

Kneel on the floor in front of a flat bench. Lay one forearm across the bench so that your palm is facing the ceiling and your wrist is at the edge of the bench, with your hand hanging over the edge. Place a small (five pounds or less) dumbbell in your hand and lower the weight over the edge of the bench, rolling the dumbbell to your fingertips at the bottom of the movement. Next, flex your wrist until the weight is above the bench and your knuckles are pointing toward your biceps. Repeat ten to fifteen times for two to three sets on each arm.

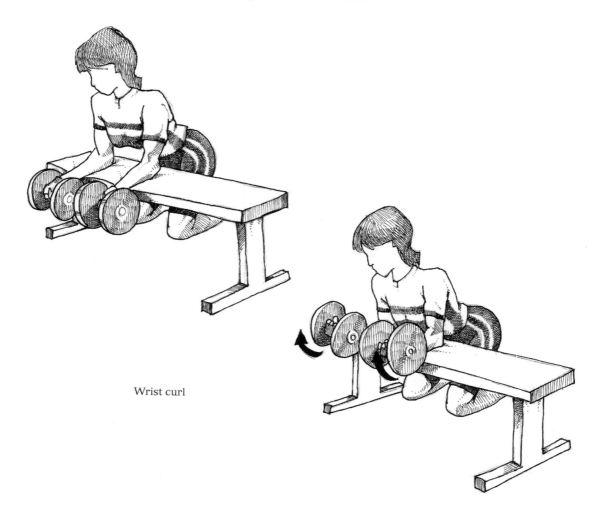

Wrist curl

Shoulders

Dumbbell press. The shoulders take the bulk of the abuse dished out by rough terrain. Having strong shoulders will increase your ability to take this abuse and will also help in explosive power moves, like popping a wheelie to cross a ditch.

Sit on a bench that has an upright backrest at one end. An incline bench that has an adjustable backrest will work well if the backrest is elevated to its most upright position. Sit on the bench with your back flat against the backrest and a pair of light (each weighing 5 to 10 percent of your body weight) dumbbells.

Grasp one in each hand with your palms facing you. Lift one dumbbell straight up, directly overhead. As you lift the dumbbell turn your fist so that at the top of the movement your palm is facing away from you. Lower the dumbbell slowly, turning your fist so that your palm is once again facing you at the bottom of the movement. At the same time lift the other dumbbell overhead in the same manner as the first. Continue to alternate, one dumbbell up, the other down, until you've completed ten to twelve reps. Increase the weight for the following two sets so that you are barely able to finish the eighth rep of the second set.

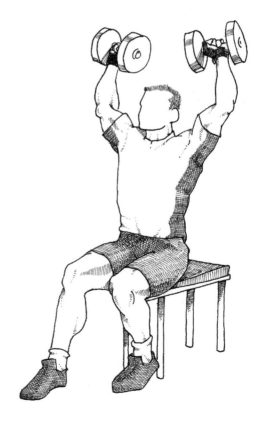

Dumbbell press

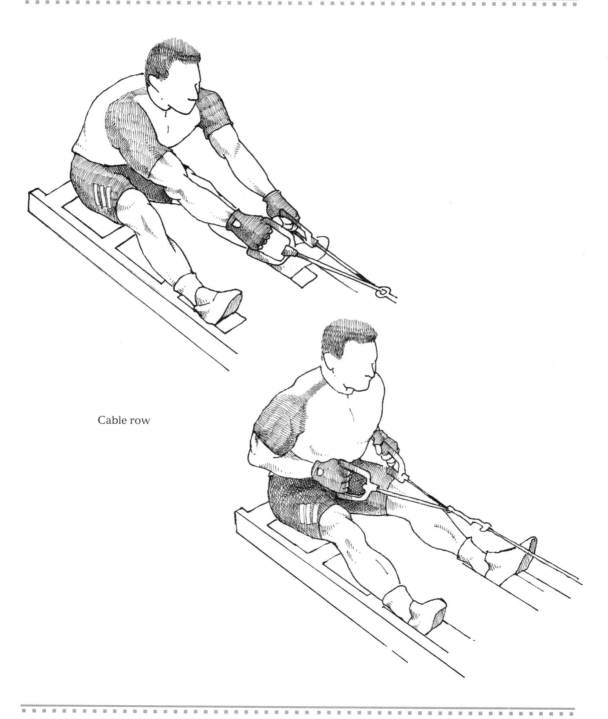

Cable row

Back

Cable rows. Strong back muscles will help in any situation that requires you to pull the handlebars toward your body, like bunny hopping, log jumping, and wheelies.

Try cable rows to strengthen your back muscles. Nearly all gyms have machines called cable row machines. They are either part of a multistation machine (usually called a Universal) or a stand-alone unit. The machine consists of a stack of weights attached to a cable that extends from the machine at floor level. The amount of weight is adjustable by moving the pin that attaches the weights to the cable.

Sit on the floor with your legs extended and your feet on a sturdy piece of wood or other material to give you something to create space between you and the machine. The cable should be at the midline of your body as you face the machine. There's a special bar, or sometimes a pair of handles, that attach to the cable. Once again, choose a light weight for your first set (about 25 percent of body weight). Grasp the handles on the cable (you should have to reach for it, down by your feet) and pull the handle to your chest as you pull back. Think of it as seated toe-touching with the added resistance of the weight on the cable. At the bottom of each movement you should be leaning forward as far as possible with your arms fully extended. At the top of each movement you should be sitting erect with your back straight and the handles of the cable at your chest. To avoid lower-back strain, don't let your back pass the upright position at the top of the movement.

LOWER BODY

The muscle group of the lower body is the machine that powers your bike. These muscles do receive training and strengthening as a result of riding. If you have to miss a workout because of a busy schedule, this is the one to skip.

Quads/Lower Back

The squat is one of the great weight-lifting exercises of all time. Squats alone will exercise most of the lower body, including the quads, hips, hamstrings, calves, lower back, and even the intercostals, the muscles between your ribs that are responsible for chest expansion.

Perform your squats in front of a full-length mirror. This will help ensure that you are maintaining proper body position, a consideration especially important in squats. Squat racks are designed to raise the bar off the floor so that you can load the bar and rest it on your shoulders without having to bend over and lift the bar from the floor. Always use a squat rack. An experienced spotter is another important component of safe squatting.

Load the squat rack with a weight that is 20 to 30 percent of your body weight. Don't forget to include the weight of the bar. Use a foam pad on the bar for protection from pinching where it will rest on your shoulders. Back up to the bar and rest it high on your shoulders, across the back of your lower neck. Grasp the bar firmly with your hands at shoulder width. If you have it in the right spot it will rest there easily without falling off. Step away from the rack and with your head held high, look at a spot on the wall above the level of your head (this is extremely important in order for squats to be safe and effective). With your feet shoulder-width apart and toes pointed slightly outward, bend your knees until your thighs are parallel to the floor. Pause for a moment and return to the upright position. Be sure to keep your head up and your back straight or slightly arched (but never hunched or rounded). Lower the weight slowly, under control, and make sure your spotter is positioned behind you following the bar up and down with you, ready to help with the weight at any time. Stick with this low weight until you are comfortable performing squats. If you have any back problems avoid squatting; choose other leg exercises instead.

Squat

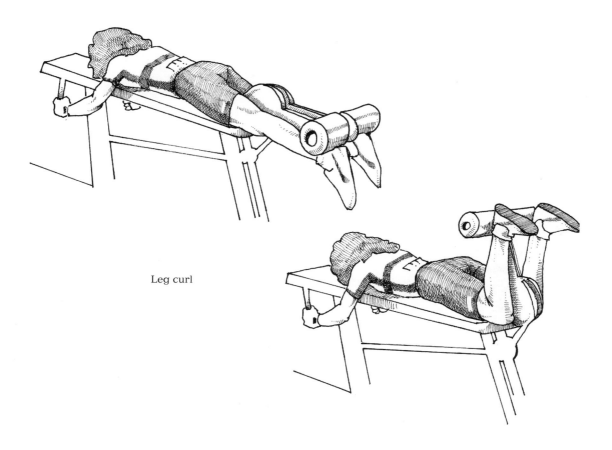

Leg curl

Hamstrings

As mentioned earlier in this chapter, an imbalance in the strength of the quads and the hamstrings can cause knee problems. Strengthen your hamstrings to prevent future problems.

Leg curls are performed at a machine that looks like a regular bench with two large rollers at the end of it. The "rollers" are where you place your feet while using this machine. Similar to the cable row machine, the leg curl machine has a weight stack with a cable at-

tached. The cable is attached to the foot piece via a pulley.

Select a weight of 10 to 15 percent of your body weight and lie face down on the bench. Hook the back of your ankles and pull the pads up in an arc toward your butt. Resist the urge to jerk the weight and move slowly and deliberately, both up and down, through the full range of motion. Repeat ten to fifteen times and increase the weight for the following two sets as outlined above.

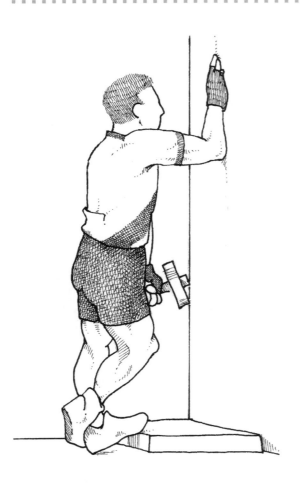

Calf raise

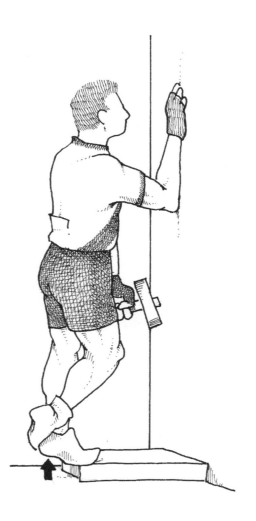

Calves

The calves are one of the toughest muscles in the body. Full of very tightly packed muscle fibers, the calves can lift several times the body weight of a strong individual. The calves are important to mountain bikers, especially during long climbs and extended periods out of the saddle.

Stand facing the wall with a medium-size (ten to twenty pounds) dumbbell in one hand. Place a 2 × 4- or 4 × 4-inch piece of wood, nailed to a larger flat board, against the wall at your feet. Step onto the 2 × 4, balancing on the ball of the foot on the same side as the dumbbell. Lift the other foot off the floor so all your weight is on this one foot. Push up with your foot until you are standing on the tips of your toes. Pause for a moment, then lower the foot so that your heel is at the bottom of the board, on the floor, and your toes are still on top of the board. Repeat ten to twenty times for three sets on each foot.

There are many exercises equivalent to the ones I've mentioned for numerous home exercise machines. If you're training with machines, either at home or in the gym, check with the staff at the gym or the training guide you received with your equipment, or consult a strength-training book.

Set goals for yourself, whether it's bench pressing a certain weight or achieving a lower resting heart rate. It's easier to make progress when you know where you're going. Use short-term goals, but also keep your sights on the big picture, whether it's an ideal body weight or the ability to ride to the top of a mountain. Imagine yourself as you'd like to be—a lean, mean mountain biking machine.

INTERVAL TRAINING

Interval training helps you raise your anaerobic threshold, which can increase endurance and improve your ability to sprint up steep hills and difficult sections of trail. Intervals are not for everyone, and are not essential to improving your aerobic fitness. But if you want to challenge yourself and see real results in your ability to maintain high-effort riding, intervals can be a big help.

Interval training involves two phases: the work interval and the rest, or recovery, interval. The work interval is a near-maximal effort of short duration, and is followed by the moderate effort rest interval. You can incorporate interval training techniques into your weekly riding routine. After warming up at a moderate pace, pour it on for fifteen to ninety seconds. When you're in the work interval, your heart rate should be near your maximum rate. After fifteen to ninety seconds, back off to allow your heart rate to drop. Ride at this level for thirty to sixty seconds and then start another work interval phase. Repeat until you have completed about ten cycles of work and recovery intervals.

Start out by sticking to fifteen-second work intervals followed by sixty-second recovery intervals and work your way up. You should be just barely able to complete the work interval in the allotted time. If you're able to maintain the effort of a work interval for more than ninety seconds, you need to work harder. If you cannot maintain the effort for even fifteen seconds, you're pushing too hard and should back off until you develop more strength.

Again, riding big hills is the easiest way to

include intervals in your training. Alternating sprints with slower intervals in a climb is challenging and produces results. Include interval training in one or two workouts per week.

STRETCHING AND WARMING UP

Each morning at the Mountain Bike School, instructors lead students through a stretching and warmup routine. Before we begin with the stretching we ask students to either do 100 jumping jacks or ride their bikes around the parking lot for five to ten minutes. Warming up before stretching brings blood and oxygen to the muscles, preparing them for the stretching that follows.

Stretching is essential to prevent muscle soreness and joint injuries, and ensures that muscles and joints can move through their full range of motion. Mountain biking is a demanding sport; it's essential to be limber and flexible to be ready for unexpected dabs or falls.

Tight ligaments are prone to injury. Say you're riding along and you unexpectedly hit a rock with your front wheel. You start to go over the handlebars and instinctively throw out your left leg in an attempt to prevent the fall. Your leg twists, stressing your knee. If your knee ligaments are tight, the stress stretches them to the limit and beyond. The result can be a torn ligament. Torn knee ligaments are probably the most common athletic injury and can result in surgery and a lifetime of problems.

A flexible knee, however, can much better handle the stress of the unexpected. Instead of tearing the ligament, you'll get a much less serious sprain or stretched tissue; if you're lucky, you may escape injury altogether.

I'd like to share some stretches I use before every ride. When stretching, move slowly with steady force. Never bounce at the bottom of a stretch.

Quads. Stand next to a wall or post and steady yourself with your left hand. Bend your knee and lift your right foot toward your butt. Grasp

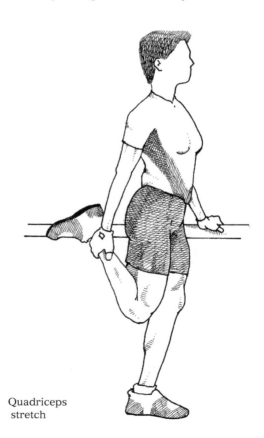

Quadriceps stretch

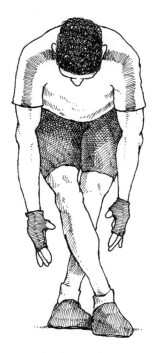

Hamstring/lower back stretch

Calves. Put your arms in front of you and with your palms flat, lean your upper body against a wall with your feet about 12 inches away from the bottom of the wall. Stand on your tippy-toes and push your right heel toward the floor. Feel the stretch in your calf muscle. Move slowly and deliberately and hold your heel at the bottom for a count of 10. Repeat ten times on each leg.

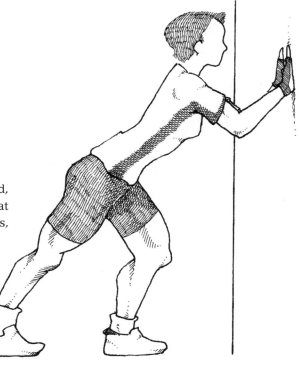

your right ankle with your right hand and, while bending forward at the waist, pull so that your upper leg moves back. Repeat ten times, then do the same with the left leg.

Hamstring/Lower Back. Cross your right foot in front of your left and reach for your toes. It's not necessary to touch your toes; just go as low as you are comfortable with and hold at the bottom for a count of 5. Repeat ten times. Cross your left foot in front of your right and repeat.

Calf stretch

Upper Back, Shoulders, Arms. Stand with your legs 12 inches apart. Clasp your hands behind your back and while bending forward at the waist move your hands directly upward, toward the sky.

Neck. Standing with your feet 12 inches apart, rest your chin on your chest. Move your head in an arc to the right until you are looking toward your right, across your right shoulder. Return to the center and repeat on the left.

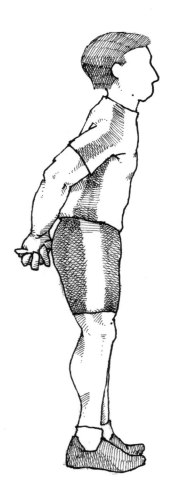

Upper back/shoulder stretch

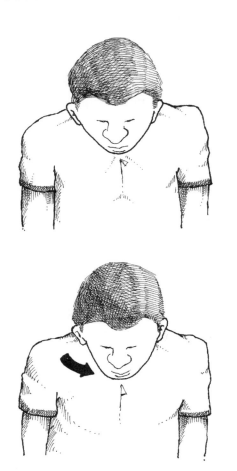

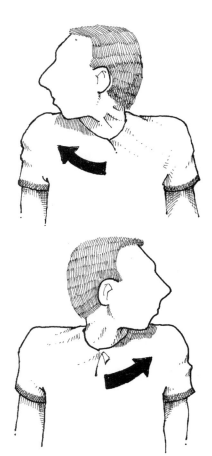

Neck roll

Complete the movement ten times. Don't move your head back farther than 90 degrees on either side and make sure the movement is slow and steady. Rapid swinging of the head and neck can cause pulled neck muscles. Remember, riding stresses your neck and shoulders, and you must work to keep these areas relaxed.

REST

Now you know about the minimum training you need to achieve results. But it's also possible to do too much. Your body needs rest to adapt and get stronger. Rest is probably the most overlooked component of training. A body that doesn't get enough rest will not be able to muster the resources it needs to repair and strengthen.

Overtraining is the result of too much exercise and not enough rest. Symptoms of overtraining are an elevated resting rate, chronic fatigue, and often difficulty sleeping. If you notice any of these you're probably overtrained. Take a week off. Catch up on your letter writing, knit a sweater, rent the entire back catalog of Marx Brothers movies. Just stay away from your bike and the gym. An overtrained body won't repair itself properly, and the exercise you give it will not improve performance. The only way to get over it is to stop.

One of my biggest challenges over the years has been recognizing when I'm overtrained and being able to stay away from my bike long enough to get the rest I need. If a friend calls and wants to go for a ride, or if it's the most beautiful day of the year, I'm hard-pressed to say no. If you must ride, take it easy and don't stay out for more than two hours.

NUTRITION

There's a story in which a young racer asks an old pro how the youngster can train to be the best biker he can. The old-timer says: "Eat a lot of spaghetti and go fast." It's an oversimplification, but a story with a large grain of truth. A training program cannot succeed without proper nutrition, which provides the body with the essential raw materials needed to maintain and repair itself.

Mountain bikers want foods that will fuel us for the demands of the trail. A diet rich in whole grains and low in fat is the ideal. Actually, it's the same stuff we're told to eat by the American Cancer Society, weight-loss experts, and cardiac specialists. But if we ride enough, we can get away with eating more of it. A lot more.

There are four ingredients essential to a balanced, high-energy diet:

WATER

Fifty to 60 percent of normal body weight is water. Water is the medium by which nutrients are distributed, waste is removed, and temperature is maintained. A deficit of water in your body will make all these functions suffer.

Strenuous exercise produces heat. When you heat up you begin to sweat. The evaporation of sweat on your skin cools the body, thereby maintaining a healthy body core temperature. Unfortunately, sweating heavily also results in significant water loss. If fluids are not replaced, serious problems can develop. Think of it this way: Your blood is essentially water with various cells floating around in it. Some of these cells (the red ones) are responsible for carrying oxygen to the muscles and vital organs. When you're dehydrated there's less water available. Less water means less blood volume. Less blood volume means less oxygen is being delivered to the muscles and vital organs. Less oxygen means less energy, and impaired performance.

Combine dehydration with heat and you can expect serious medical problems. Heatstroke, for example, is the condition that results in dangerously elevated core body temperature. When body fluids are seriously

Eat right for maximum energy and endurance.

depleted, the body stops sweating in an attempt to preserve water for vital organ functions. Since the mechanism for cooling the body is interrupted, body temperature climbs rapidly. The skin takes on a flushed, dry character and, if unchecked, unconsciousness and death can result.

A person who appears to be suffering from heatstroke requires immediate, qualified medical attention. It may signal a life-threatening situation. If possible, whisk the person to a cool place out of the sun and cool the body with a wet cloth, a T-shirt, or other clothing. Do not give food or drink to someone who may be suffering from heatstroke.

The other heat exposure–related condition

is called heat shock. A less serious condition than heat stroke, it's nonetheless potentially dangerous. Riders suffering from heat shock will exhibit cool, pale, damp skin, chills, and nausea. Once again, get the person out of the sun and give him or her small amounts of water. While this condition's not usually life-threatening, it's probably best to seek nonbike transportation for the rider.

Prevent these situations by drinking plenty of water before, during, and after exercise. I like to drink as much water as possible before I go for a ride. In order to be fully hydrated you should begin drinking plenty of water twenty-four to thirty-six hours before exercise. This means that if you exercise on a regular basis, you need to be drinking plenty of water all the time, not just when you're riding. This is true whether it's 10 degrees or 90 degrees outside. In warm weather you should drink at least one pint of water an hour during exercise. Don't wait until you're thirsty to drink; by this time you're already on your way to becoming dehydrated. Plan on carrying the water you need, or find out where water is available on the trail.

Electrolyte replacement, or sports drinks, can help boost endurance in warm weather. Use sports drinks when your ride is more than ninety minutes. When you sweat, your salts, also called electrolytes, are depleted. Salts such as sodium chloride (table salt) and potassium are essential in regulating the amount of fluids retained by the body, and are also important in the functioning of the muscles. Replacing lost electrolytes while we ride helps keep our bodies functioning optimally. Eat salty foods during long rides (five hours or more) to help your body regulate the amount of stored fluids.

CARBOHYDRATES

Carbohydrates are found in sugars (simple carbohydrates) and in starchy foods such as bread and potatoes (complex carbohydrates). The body converts carbohydrates into glycogen, a sugar stored in the liver and muscles. Glycogen is an important ingredient in maintaining the body's basic functions (it's what our brains run on), as well as being an essential fuel during intense exercise. Whole-grain foods, such as oats, trail mix, and whole-grain breads, are rich in complex carbohydrates. Eat plenty of these foods prior to a big ride to store as much glycogen as possible.

While stored glycogen is essential in optimal performance, it's also important to maintain your blood sugar levels during exercise. Eat snacks at least every two hours while riding. Half an energy bar may be all you need, but frequent snacks of complex carbohydrates, like trail mix, energy bars, carbohydrate energy drinks, and fruit, will maintain blood sugar levels and prevent the dreaded "bonk," the equivalent of a physical power brownout. Bonking will leave you tired, hungry, and very cranky. Try fixing a flat when you're bonking and don't have any food; it's not pretty. I've seen crazed bonksters throw their bikes over cliffs, relationships on the verge of collapse, murder in the eyes of Smokey the Bear.

It's also important to restore your glycogen levels after a big effort. Once again, eat plenty of whole-grain foods to rebuild your reserves.

PROTEIN

Dietary protein is necessary in maintaining tissue health and muscle mass. Proteins are not stored, so it's important to eat protein on a regular basis in order to maintain your muscles, skin, and other organs. Amino acids are a component of proteins used by the body to manufacture body proteins such as skin and muscle. Nine of these are considered essential, since they cannot be manufactured by the body and must be obtained through the diet.

Meat, fish, poultry, and dairy products offer complete proteins containing all nine essential amino acids. Vegetable proteins are incomplete, lacking one or more of the essential amino acids. If you're a vegetarian, it's important to combine incomplete proteins—for example, rice and beans—to get all the amino acids you need to maintain healthy muscles and skin.

FATS

Fats are an important part of our diets. Fats are needed for maintenance of cellular functions and can be an important source of energy—especially in cold environments. The problem is that the typical American's diet is too rich in fats for the amount of energy expended, resulting in an increased incidence of obesity and heart disease.

Avoid foods high in saturated fats, like butter and lard. (Darn, do I really have to give up lard?) Instead, eat a moderate amount of foods containing mono- and polyunsaturated fats. These oils can actually reduce the amount of cholesterol in your blood. Be careful, though;

they have every bit as many calories as saturated fats, and calories are calories, no matter where they come from.

A well-balanced, high-energy diet should contain about 60 percent carbohydrates, 15 percent protein, and 25 percent fat. In other words, if you're eating 2,500 calories a day, 1,500 of those calories should come from carbohydrates, 375 from protein, and 625 from fat. Luckily, recent food labeling regulations have made it much easier to calculate the number of calories from each of these in a particular food product. Read labels and know what you're eating.

It's not necessary to spend gobs of money on dietary supplements to get all the nutrients you need. So-called muscle-building powders with all kinds of designer proteins are expensive, and since proteins are not stored, your money is literally going down the toilet. Instead, take a sensible, smart approach and look to the foods you eat to maintain health and boost performance.

MOTIVATION

I have no mantras, affirmations, or chants to keep you motivated. But I do have one word that should keep you going, even when the going gets tough: *fun*. If you make mountain biking fun, the rest will come easily. Ride with friends. Find new trails. Learn about local wildlife. Pick a section of trail that you have trouble with and ride it over and over until you get it right. Set goals for yourself. Make them modest at first so that they are easily attainable. Do whatever it takes to ride consistently.

SAMPLE TRAINING WEEK

It's not absolutely necessary to chart out your training week by week. As a matter of fact, if you're too wedded to a particular regime you're setting yourself up for failure when you miss a workout. Instead, use a training schedule as a guide for what you'd like to accomplish in a given week. If you can't get away from your day-to-day life to ride on Wednesday, then ride on Thursday. Get a lighting system so you can ride at night. By having as many options as possible you can adapt to the trials of modern life without sacrificing the consistency necessary to make progress. Be flexible, and don't beat yourself up when you miss a workout; that will serve only to frustrate and impede motivation.

It's also important not to do too much. Ned Overend (six-time national cross-country champion) wasn't built in a day. Overplanning sets you up for failure, so keep it realistic and make sure you can fit it into the schedule of your day-to-day life.

I like to ride in the morning best. In the summer it's the coolest part of the day, and I like to get my training over with so that I can spend the rest of the day doing what I have to do and feeling great because of the workout I've had. You should ride when *you* want. Do whatever works best for you. Some people can't even think in complete sentences in the morning. If you're reluctantly dragging your butt out to ride in the morning, or if, on the other hand, you can't focus on anything during the day until you've had your ride (that's me), then you're not going to get the most out of your workout.

MONDAY: Hill climb

TUESDAY: Strength training; Fun ride

WEDNESDAY: Intervals

THURSDAY: Strength training; Road ride

FRIDAY: Rest day

SATURDAY: Four- to six-hour endurance ride

SUNDAY: Fun ride

You'll notice a couple of things about the way I've set up this sample week. First, I've included two fun rides. This means ride without a training agenda. Help a novice who's just learning, ride with a local group to do trail maintenance, forget about your training, and have fun. One of the most frustrating experiences is to have to wait for a slower rider when you're trying to keep moving. Don't mix training with casual riding—it's not fair to you or to the others in your group. Instead, set aside specific times for mixed group riding and save your training rides for yourself and others who ride at your ability level.

I also like to include one day of complete rest. It's essential that you spend at least one day recuperating, otherwise you'll find yourself overtrained.

I've also included a road ride. This can be on either a road bike or a mountain bike. The idea is to get out and work on your spin. On the road you can pick a good cadence (90 rpm) and hold it there for an extended period of time. Hone your spinning skills on the road and you'll be more effective on the trail.

An endurance ride of four to six hours once a week will boost your ability to maintain effort for long periods of time. Your body gets used to its routine. If your rides are always of short duration (two to four hours), then this will be a long ride as far as your body is concerned. Add a long ride and your shorter rides will become easier.

SIX WAYS TO MAKE YOUR TRAINING MORE EFFECTIVE

1. BE CONSISTENT

To make substantial progress in your training, it's essential above all else to be consistent in your training sessions. While I do believe it's important to be flexible in your schedule, if you miss too many workouts your progress will suffer. In order to make significant gains you must train regularly, a minimum of three days a week, forty minutes a day.

Commit to a level of training you can live with; don't become overambitious and vow to ride and train every day. That will lead to over-training—the cause of many an abandoned training regimen. Commit instead to a high-intensity aerobic workout three or four days a week and two or three days of strength training in the gym. This will mean a total time commitment of eight to fifteen hours a week—time I'm sure you've spent on worse things.

2. GET YOUR REST

It takes plenty of rest for your body to rebuild itself after the stresses you've put on it. The principle of training, aerobic or strength, is to stress your body through exercise and then let your body rebuild itself. When your body does its rebuilding, it anticipates additional demands to be put on it and becomes stronger. Through a progressive program you can create truly incredible changes in your levels of strength and fitness. Without proper rest, however, your body won't have the resources it needs to rebuild. That's why you never exercise the same group of muscles on consecutive days in weight training.

3. BE ADAPTABLE

While mountain biking is my primary means of cardiovascular exercise, I often incorporate other aerobic activities. If I had to depend on good mountain biking weather to get my aerobic exercise, I'd never be able to achieve the consistency necessary to maintain my aerobic capacity.

So whenever the mountain biking isn't that great, or when I feel like a change of pace, I substitute another activity. If the water is warm and the weather's nice, I swim; if it's rainy or I'm traveling without my bike, I run. In winter, when I'm not ice riding, I love to cross-country ski on the same trails where I mountain bike in the summer. Come spring, when the trails are muddy but the days are warm and dry, I ride my road bike. Sometimes, just for fun, I race the biking portion of a triathlon relay with a couple of friends. The more aerobic activities you add to your repertoire, the more you're able to adapt. This will give you fewer missed workouts and better training results.

Cross-training is a many-splendored thing. Varying your activities will produce a more well-rounded fitness. More muscles are exercised in more ways. Muscles and joints that are highly stressed during one activity will get rest while doing another. Along with regular stretching, this will help prevent injuries.

4. Be Smart

Read everything you can get your hands on about training. Read mountain bike magazines, talk to your friends, learn more about nutrition.

5. Stay Wet

Many athletes, amateur and professional, let themselves get underhydrated. Whenever I go for a ride, whether it's the hottest day of the year or the coldest, I start drinking water a couple of hours before I leave and bring plenty on the trail with me. On a long ride on a hot day, one bottle won't do much for you.

6. Find a Partner

Finding someone to train with can keep you motivated and make training less tedious. It helps to have someone to chat and exchange training ideas with; when you've made arrangements to meet someone for a ride, it's also less likely you'll skip going.

7

· · · · ·

CHILL OUT

Off-Season and Winter Riding

If you live in an area with four seasons, it's wonderful to watch the year go by on a mountain bike. You see each cycle unfold and blend into the next. When the leaves turn to gold and skis and snowboards come out of the closet around the country, my mind turns to . . . riding my bike at night in subfreezing temperatures, on bulletproof ice. Winter, especially, offers exhilarating riding—if you prepare properly. When snow and silence blanket everything, the terrain becomes incredibly beautiful.

In a more practical vein, winter riding keeps you in shape by extending your season. Come spring, you won't have to start your training from scratch. Your rides won't be as long, and you probably won't ride as often as during the warm months, but at least you'll retain much of what you accomplished the previous season. Many road bikers take to mountain biking in the winter to maintain their training schedule. Since mountain bikes travel at much slower

speeds than road bikes, there's less windchill.

Sometimes, I even turn winter jaunts into excursions that provide a whole different experience. I bring matches, bread, and cheese; stop halfway through my ride to toast myself a grilled cheese sandwich; and eat lunch by the fire. Like most of mountain biking, cold-weather riding is all attitudinal. If you tell yourself you're going to be miserable, you will. If you tell yourself you're going to have a good time, you will. So just relax, be careful, and enjoy yourself.

Ice riding opens you up to other experiences. You become more willing to take risks and make yourself vulnerable, less hesitant to put yourself in uncertain situations. You trust yourself more. You learn how to stay in control—and when it's OK not to be in control.

Off-season riding also opens you up to a multidimensional relationship with terrain. If you hide the bike when it gets cold, and you don't ski or do anything else, you're experienc-

ing only one aspect of the landscape. Part of the challenge of the sport is pushing your limits—and your bike's. That's the idea behind ice riding, snowtire slaloms, and other ostensibly insane activities. Whatever the parameters of your experience, you'll always be pushing the old limits and discovering new ones to surmount and surpass. You can do it on several levels—endurance, weather, whatever.

Weather conditions, of course, vary according to where you live. In the coastal Northeast, there's a long period with no snow in the winter. Cold temperatures, rather than cold conditions, are the thing that's different from the

rest of the year. You can probably ride most of the season on dirt, especially from the Middle Atlantic to down south.

Obviously, you won't mountain bike all winter. But ice riding at least gives you the option of taking advantage of all of it and the feeling of having that possibility is wonderful. It's empowering. It expands your perception of where you live. You need to take just a little extra care to ensure that your bike—and you—function optimally in cold weather. You have to become conscientious about what you eat, how you dress, and how cold weather might affect your particular bike.

CLOTHING

Cycling in cold weather (45 degrees or less) has always been a challenge. The problem is that you start out cold, then warm up and break a sweat, which makes you wet. Then, while going downhill, the combination of wet skin and windchill makes for a truly bone-chilling experience. Clothing manufacturers have responded by inventing various kinds (mostly knit polyesters) of space-age fabrics designed to wick the moisture away from your body and into the outer layers of clothing, where it's released into the air through evaporation, thereby keeping you warm and dry.

Sounds pretty good, huh? The problem is that while these fabrics really do make this kind of winter activity possible, they're not perfect. If you climb a big hill and work up a major sweat, you'll still be wet when you get to the top, no matter what you do. Be ready to shed a layer or two, if you get too warm. It's OK to be a little chilly at first; you'll warm up once you get going.

There are three basic layers to wear while riding in cold conditions. First, wear a layer of polypropylene next to your skin, then an insulating layer of polyester fleece or other material that has a nap to capture an insulating layer of air. On top of all this wear a breathable wind-resistant shell. Unless it's very cold (20 degrees or less) you probably can skip the middle layer on your legs. Experiment with different weight fabrics for different temperatures. Make sure your torso is well insulated, as this is where your core body temperature is regulated. If your core is warm, then it's more likely your extremities will also be warm.

Here's a list of cold weather riding accessories:

Booties. Your feet are probably the most vulnerable part of your body in cold temperatures. The pressure of pedaling tends to cut off circulation to your toes, which can put you at risk for frostbite. Neoprene booties are a must in subfreezing conditions. You can find neoprene overboots in most bike mail-order catalogs. They zip on over your cycling shoes and have a pattern in the sole where you can cut out a piece to accommodate cleats.

Gloves. Several manufacturers make "lobster gloves," a mitten-glove hybrid that separates the index finger and thumb from the rest of your hand. They're warmer than regular gloves, and the distinct index finger allows you to operate your shifter and brake levers. Carry a pair of lightweight polypropylene glove liners as a backup if your hands get cold. If you have to stop to take care of a minor repair, liners can protect you from the cold while allowing you the dexterity needed.

Glasses. Wraparound glasses that provide maximum wind protection are best to protect the eyes and prevent tearing, more of a problem in cold temperatures than in warm. As we mentioned in chapter 5, glasses with interchangeable lenses of varying darkness will prepare you for dusk and darkness. Again, stick with shatterproof plastic.

Socks. Wear heavy socks, but be careful not to have too much bulk. An overly heavy sock will make your shoes tight, cut off circulation, and

Having the right equipment is especially important
in cold temperatures.

make your feet cold. Try socks made for cross-country skiing; they're warm, lightweight, and ride high on the calf, offering a little extra protection. If you feel you need to have an extra layer, silk ski socks are very warm, also extremely lightweight, and won't add much bulk.

Underwear. Polypropylene is the best and is available in various weights. Lightweight is best for temperatures above freezing (32 to 50 degrees), while heavier weights are necessary for colder temperatures.

Insulating layer. Polypropylene fleece is the best. Like underwear, it's available in various weights. You can probably skip this layer in temperatures over 50 degrees, but may need two insulating layers in very cold conditions (20 degrees or less).

Wind protection. Moving air is the main cause of body heat loss. Good wind protection will allow you to vent perspiration while protecting you from windchill. Most wind-protection gear is made of nylon laminated with a wind-resistant material. Choose a jacket and pants based on durability, breathability, and price, as this sort of clothing can be quite expensive. If you ride in traffic, at dusk, or at night, find an outfit that incorporates reflective material to make you more visible to motorists.

Helmet, liner, and cover. Your mother always told you that 50 percent of your body heat is lost through your head; she was right. Helmets are designed to be cool in the summer, not warm in the winter. Fleece helmet liners com-

bined with wind-resistant covers can keep your head and ears warm in cold temperatures.

FOOD AND DRINK

When it's cold outside your body has to work harder at staying warm. When you bonk in cold weather it's not just uncomfortable, it's outright dangerous. Blood sugars fuel the body, allowing it to maintain its temperature. Always bring lots of high-energy food, like energy bars (carry them close to your body so you don't break your teeth!) or trail mix. I'm serious when I say that food can mean the difference between life and death in cold temperatures.

Don't forget to drink plenty of water before you go out. Even though you may not feel thirsty in cold weather, it's just as important to stay well hydrated. Drink as much as you can, starting several hours before you ride. Exposed to the elements, water freezes easily in a water bottle cage, and drinking very cold water can lower your body temperature.

EQUIPMENT

Cables, derailleurs, and brakes. When temperatures dip below freezing, even without snow, it's imperative to avoid moisture on your bike. Don't slosh through puddles or get the bike wet. If cables get wet and freeze, your bike won't work; if your derailleur ices up, your gears won't shift properly; if your rims get glazed with a layer of ice, your brakes won't work. Ride around puddles, or walk the bike around them if necessary.

Once you realize that parts have begun freezing up, let them freeze fully before you chip off the ice. Wiping ice will just spread moisture, and it will freeze almost immediately, anyway. An aerosol lubricant can help melt the ice completely after you chip it off. Water in your cable housings can make life very difficult for even the most plucky mountain biker. You'll

Studded tires are like crampons for mountain bikes. *(Photo by Mike Piniewski)*

have to take the bike inside, warm it up, and dry it out before you can ride again.

Tires. Studded tires can be fun, even essential, when riding after snowy or icy weather. The traction that studs provide on glazed surfaces is truly astonishing. There are a few brands of studded mountain bike tires available commercially, although the best are made at home. Pick a tire with big, square lugs. Choose a sheet metal screw from your local hardware store that will protrude ¼ to ½ inch when screwed through the center of the lug from the inside of the tire. Phillips head screws installed with an electric driver work best. Stainless-steel screws will last longer and won't rust. Predrill each lug, then install the sheet metal screws.

You must line the tire to prevent the screw heads from giving you a flat. I've found that an old tube with the valve removed, cut open on the inside circumference, wrapped around the new tube, and held in place with electrical tape (use electrical tape because it will stretch as you inflate the tube) to be very effective. Avoid riding your studs on pavement, as this will quickly wear the screws down, significantly reducing the life of your tires.

Pedals. If you're planning to ride through snow, get rid of your clipless pedals. Cleats and release mechanisms get fouled easily in snow and won't work properly. If you want to pedal through soft snow, dig out your old bear-trap pedals from the closet.

Suspension. If you have air-oil suspension, it's possible to replace the oil with a lighter viscosity oil. Summer-weight oil thickens at cold temperatures, limiting the functionality of the system. It won't hurt to leave the oil that's in there, but don't expect the same shock absorption as you get in the summer. If you're riding on snow and ice, it probably doesn't matter. But if you're riding on primarily the same type of terrain as in the summer, just at colder temperatures, you may want to change to a lighter oil.

Temperatures affect elastomer suspension much less. Still, you may want to experiment with softer bumpers if you feel the ride is too stiff. Check with your mechanic about custom tuning your suspension for winter riding.

SPECIAL RIDING CONSIDERATIONS

Snow. Ride snow as you would any other soft surface. Keep your weight back to keep the front wheel light; this will help the bike track better. It can also help to increase your cadence to about 100 rpm. This will allow you to power through especially soft sections more easily.

Very deep, soft snow is not rideable—period. Your tires will sink right into it and bog down. Look for packed snow instead; snowmobile trails offer miles of it (not all snowmobilers welcome bikers on their trails; always ask the landowner's permission). Stay away from cross-country ski trails, no matter how good they look. A tire rut on a cross-country trail will grab a ski and can hurt someone.

Ice. Once you get all your equipment set, ice riding is really a breeze. Traction is so good with studded tires that you can get away with almost anything. Keep alert for hidden holes or cracks in the ice that could catch your tires and dump you off your bike. A hard fall on ice can result in serious injury.

NIGHT RIDING

Riding your bike at night is a truly other-worldly experience. Terrain you've ridden a thousand times becomes strange and mysterious. There's nothing like riding on a clear starry night, stopping to switch off your light and gaze at the Milky Way.

When riding at night, especially in the winter, take it easy. The angle of the light is very low compared to sunlight and the way shadows fall can do strange things with depth perception, making small depressions in the trail look like major holes and making big holes almost invisible. Low-hanging branches may also be invisible. Wear eye protection; most sunglasses with interchangeable lenses are available with a clear lens. Ride terrain you're familiar with; it's very easy to get lost at night, since your whole world is contained in the area illuminated by your light. Plan short rides.

Lighting. There are numerous systems on the market, everything from Velcro straps that hold an ordinary flashlight on your handlebars to high-tech halogen systems costing as much as $300. If you plan on riding at night, make sure that the system you've chosen will adequately illuminate the terrain. A flashlight sys-

Night riding can add adventure to your life.

tem is probably only good enough to get you to the end of your street and back. Twelve-watt rechargeable systems with at least two hours of running time are the minimum needed to be useful. Anything less than 12 watts will not be bright enough, and less than two hours doesn't give you enough leeway if you have problems on the trail.

For mounting, handlebars work well, as does helmet mounting or a combination of the two. However, since helmet-mounted lights illuminate the trail on the same plane as your line of sight, you won't see any shadows, so your depth perception will be impaired. Use a handlebar-mounted light in conjunction with your helmet light. This will improve your ability to see obstacles clearly.

Always carry a backup system, even if it's only a mini-flashlight. Rechargeable systems can be fluky, and you don't want to be stuck out on the trail without any light at all.

If you have to ride on the road to get to the trail, make sure that you mount a flashing red light on the back of your bike so that motorists can see you.

SAFETY

Off-season and night riding are risky. Accepting that risk is up to you. I can't ask you to sign a release form before you read this chapter, so please use your head. Start slow. Try a thirty-minute ride and feel your way around. You may find it's not for you and that will be that.

Here are some safety tips:

1. **Avoid any ice less than 10 inches thick.** If you're not sure of the depth, stay off the ice.

2. **Don't ride at night in unfamiliar terrain.**

3. **Make sure you don't try this lunacy alone.** Ordinary safety principles become life-and-death issues in subfreezing weather. A flat tire in a remote area at night can be life-threatening.

4. **Keep your rides to two hours or less.** Fatigue can come suddenly and unexpectedly in cold weather. Never be more than an hour away from home.

5. **Use your common sense.** The safety precautions outlined in other areas of this book hold true, but your margin of error in the winter is all but eliminated. Better to overprepare than to not be ready when something unexpected happens. Have an emergency plan in case you get into trouble.

6. **Be sure someone knows where you're going and when you plan on returning.** Notify this person on your return.

■ ■ ■

Lots of times fun is waiting to happen—you just need to look for it. A few years back, I was sitting in a management meeting about winter events at Mount Snow. I wasn't paying attention, since I was waiting for my turn to talk about all the cool stuff planned for the upcoming mountain bike season. As I gazed out the window, I started daydreaming about riding my bike down the mountain—turning in the snow, schussing through slalom gates. At that very moment, a vice president jarred me from my stupor by asking the group if anyone had any ideas for new winter events.

I've never been one to think before I speak (which is generally a good thing, I think), so I blurted out, half joking, "How about a mountain bike race on snow?" I wasn't expecting anyone to take me seriously. After I said it, I thought that all I'd get out of management was a few raised eyebrows and shaking heads.

"That's a great idea!" the VP said, to my total surprise.

"Really?"

"Yes! What'll we call it?"

"How about the Snowtire Slalom?"

"Great! Write up a proposal and a budget and get it to me within a week."

That was in 1991. In 1995, the Snowtire Slalom drew more than 160 racers from all over the country. It's become one of Mount Snow's most popular winter events.

■ ■ ■

Ice

It's a moonless January night. The breeze in the bare tree branches makes a dry sound. Unlike the full rustling of summer wind, this is singular, a cold rushing. The gusts let loose ice from the branches, glazed by the latest round of freezing rain. It makes a tinkling music, its rhythm driven by waves in the air.

Eric and I have been riding for an hour now, following a single snowmobile track up the ridge. Our tires, studded with 1,476 sheet metal screws, make a clicking sound on the ice. Our lights create a bubble of vision at our front wheels. We stop after cresting the ridge and shut down the lights, deciding not to drop into the Somerset Reservoir drainage. Its lightless, uninhabited valley seems ultimately uninviting and menacing.

Even with an ambient temperature of 10 degrees Fahrenheit, we're overheated; the climb was long and steep, the track sheer, shiny ice. Turning back seems the only reasonable thing to do; to continue would be to flirt with catastrophe. The valley below has no phones, no year-round homes, only a few scattered shelters with a questionable supply of firewood. If

there were trouble of any kind, if either of us were injured, or even if it were only a flat tire, the situation could become perilous, the trip back to civilization uphill on glare ice. Better to face the trip home downhill.

On the way down my light goes dim, and I ride out in front of Eric, stealing some of his light. The snowmobile track seems steeper on the way down; the natural commonsense fear of riding a bicycle at night on ice is augmented by the terror of my light's not working. By the time we return we've chilled considerably, but I feel exhilarated, like I've been to the North Pole and back in the two hours since work.

Winters in New England of late have followed a messy and disturbing pattern. Even in the northern states rain seems more likely than snow in any given month. Ski areas struggle with cycles of rain, freezing rain, and sleet followed by periods of frigid temperatures when the world seems imprisoned in ice. Nordic ski areas can't count on having a season at all. Those of us who have built a lifestyle around snow and skiing endure weekly ordeals following weather reports hoping for snow, only to be disappointed once again by rain and the twenty-below temperatures that follow.

All that ice, all that terrain, all those discouraging weather reports now have a different quality. While my friends bemoan another cycle of icy weather I get a smug little smile on my face, because I know that conditions will be ideal for ice riding. Freezing rain turns snowmobile trails on seasonal roads into silky-smooth, hard-as-nails bike paths for sicko, never-give-up mountain bikers like myself.

Not that I don't like deep fluffy powder, mind you; I think winter should bring endless amounts of the stuff. I revel in a day on my backcountry skis, when the conditions are right. But in Vermont one has to be adaptable to enjoy the backcountry on a regular basis. Now when the snow is good, I ski; when the ice is upon us, I ride. By never having to stay indoors and miss a workout, I get the best of both worlds.

Vermont was made for mountain biking. More than half its roads are unpaved. There are also 1,500 miles of town trails and what are known as Class IV roads—seasonal roads open to the public, but largely unmaintained—the legacy of a mid–nineteenth-century farming industry that has since disappeared. In the mid-1800s, 85 percent of Vermont land was open fields and pasture; now the same percentage is wooded. Left behind is mile upon mile of abandoned roads, ideal for summer mountain bike riding, but also ideal for cross-country skiing, snowshoeing, and snowmobiling. When the ice comes and none of these activities are possible, enter the ice machine, the vicious cycle.

Kevin Harrington lives on a farm in Pawlet, Vermont. Among other endeavors, he owns Vermont Stud Service, a custom mountain bike tire-studding service. He works by himself in a small room inside an old barn warmed by a kerosene space heater. On a jig made of wood scraps, he produces the VT Stud 364, his deluxe tire with 364 screws set into the lugs of a Ritchie Fat Trax 1.9 tire. By hand, each stud is set into a predrilled hole using a power screwdriver.

Kevin has brought ice riding to the masses. He makes crampons for mountain bikes. Before I met Kevin I made my own studs. It used to take me ten hours per tire for 150 studs. Now for a modest amount of cash I get a superior product, and more important, I can spread the gospel of ice riding to my friends.

Another rainfall has turned the backcountry into a mass of ice fields. Trees stand in streams frozen, as if captured in a photograph. My friend Scott and I load my truck and head out on a cold Sunday morning, deciding on a route in Williamsville, Vermont, a tiny hamlet in the southeastern corner of the state. Arriving in Williamsville, we leave the pavement and turn onto Baker Brook Road. A year-round road for its first few miles, it becomes a Class IV road owing to its rugged terrain and remote location. We drive to the end of the plowed road and park the truck. From here the unmaintained section follows Baker Brook and climbs steeply toward Wardsboro. There's not much snow cover at this lower elevation, but the route I have in mind climbs 1,500 vertical feet. We expect to see more snow and ice as we make our ascent.

Suiting up, we pull on our neoprene booties and check for extra socks and gloves. Four peanut butter and jelly sandwiches are placed in the backpack, along with water, tools, tubes, and an extra rear derailleur—being unprepared in 15-degree weather is *not* fun. Discussing technique with Scott, a neophyte to ice riding, I advise him that everything true of summer mountain biking also applies in winter, only more so. Take your weight off the rear tire in a climb, and spin out. Fall, and you fall hard on ice. If you lose it on a pitch, you slide. Stop to make a repair, and you chill—fast.

The road ahead is flat and gray with ice. As we ride I see what's left of snowmobile tracks under my wheels. This was once snow; half an inch of rain has turned it to solid ice. Ten minutes into our ride we meet a group of four women walking toward us. They clutch at each other, trying to avoid falling on the ice. As we approach they stare in disbelief. Stopping to say hello and bask in their incredulity, we hear of their many falls. It seems odd having casual conversation in such a surreal setting. The women are beaten and humbled by the terrain. At the same time they are amazed and intrigued by our apparent conquest of the ice. "Where are you going?" "How did you make those tires?" After answering their questions I ask if the road ahead is as icy. When they answer yes, I giggle with excitement—it's going to be a good day.

The road starts to climb after half a mile. Several glazed bridges cross Baker Brook's meandering course. Soon we reach what I call the wall, a particularly steep and winding section of the road. I fell once, descending the wall at night. It was then, as now, solid edge-to-edge ice. As I slid, feet still in the toe clips, I wondered if I was headed for the twenty-foot drop into the series of waterfalls that is Baker Brook. I imagined being found in the spring, frozen fingers still clutching the brake levers. I choose not to share this experience with Scott, and suggest that if he doesn't think he can make the pitch he should head for the ditch on the other side of the road.

At the top of the wall we stop and catch our breath. Riding encumbered by all this clothing and equipment makes for hard work and sweaty armpits. The trail passes some summer cabins and turns into deeper forest, where even four-wheel drive won't get you through.

In the early 1800s this was the only road from Williamsville to Wardsboro. Now it's the end of the line unless you're a hiker or a foolish mountain biker.

There was a mill here once. The stone dam, built to hold the pond that powered the water wheel, is now breached. It sits thirty feet above the icy brook. Just downstream, a stone arch bridge crosses a ravine. Our route leads across the bridge and up the steep hill on the other side. Decades of water running down the trail has worn a fifteen-foot diameter, twenty-foot deep hole in the middle of the bridge. The most recent rain and the sudden drop in temperature (40 to 15 degrees in two hours) has left a heavy coating of ice on bridge and trail.

As we contemplate negotiating the bridge, Scott, an experienced triathlete and long-distance runner, looks more than a little nervous. A tightrope-thin line exists to cross the bridge—the hole on one side, the ravine on the other. The passage is steeply crowned, and as if that isn't enough, the hill on the other side is thick with ice. A fall and its resulting slide would lead directly down the hole, twenty feet into the brook and a tangle of ice-encrusted logs and brush.

We decide to walk, not ride, across the bridge and into the safety of some trees on the other side. Walking is not without its own perils, however, as the neoprene booties have as much traction as bedroom slippers on the ice. I go first, as if I did this every day. Reaching the other side safely, I tell Scott to hold onto his bike with the brakes locked and inch across, using the bike as an anchor. The studs are our only means of survival. Once he joins me on the other side, I ask if he had looked down the hole. Crossing this bridge I know how Dorothy felt when she got the Wicked Witch's broomstick, how Sir Edmund Hillary felt when he reached the summit of Everest. I need to look into the face of the demon to know it's been conquered. I ask Scott if he looked to find out if he sees it as I do, not to taunt him. I get only a hostile glare as a reply.

We've been out for two hours now. Before us is an eight-mile climb up the old road. In the summer it's a jumble of cobbles and exposed ledge that is marginally rideable at best. Now it's thick with ice. A constant trickle of freezing water has turned the trail into a series of terraced ice floes, one tabletop joined to another by solidified waterfalls. Motionless fingers of ice reach out at us from the banks above. Only the breeze in the trees and the calls of distant birds assure us that time has not stood still. Back on our bikes we're surprised at how easy the climb seems: the traction is flawless, as if the tires and the ice are made of Velcro. There's almost no rolling resistance on the ice, as if the woods have been paved. I get cocky and try some sprints up onto the bank, diving back down like a snowboarder on an uphill half-pipe. Behind me I hear Scott giggling his mantra over and over: "This is unbelievable."

Our goal is to reach the top of Oregon Mountain, a 2,000-foot knob looming over Williamsville. The old road approaches the top from the west and then plummets 1,500 vertical feet in 3½ miles to the sanded town road that leads back to the truck. I can see that Scott is tiring; his grin has been replaced by a look of shaky resolve. I feel drained, too, but can't let on; I know we have a while to go before we reach the top.

This is a tough ride in warm weather—twenty miles, three towns, and a lot of technical climbing. I have underestimated the draining effect of the cold and the extra gear, but at this point I can do nothing but keep us moving. Three miles from the summit Scott tells me he has a flat. We rush to fix it; no time to rest—the shadows are getting longer and I'm concerned about getting back before dark.

Finally, we reach the top of Oregon Mountain. Breaking out the last of the food, we try to suck some water out of the ice in our bottles. Scott grumbles something about how mountain biking is supposed to be fun. I sheepishly assure him that all this work will be worth the descent, and hope that I'm right.

I let Scott go down first, feeling better being able to keep an eye on him. The ice floe exceeds my expectations. It's longer, steeper, more extensive than anything I've ever seen. Sheets of thick ice blanket the forest floor. Scott and I ride side-by-side, a dual slalom in the trees. Suddenly the ice caves in under my front wheel and I'm catapulted over the handlebars. The recent rain has undermined the ice already on the trail. Newly frozen, it gave no clue to its hollow nature. Sliding, I grab for a tree to keep out of the brook below. The bike clatters by on its own, and comes to rest against a rock.

Regaining my composure, I assure Scott that I'm OK and we continue our descent. The ice seems never-ending. Its mirror-smooth surface has an organic shape—*The Blob That Ate Williamsville.* Looking down I see leaves and twigs perfectly preserved in crystal orbs of ice, the afternoon sun tinting them a soft orange. Ahead, Scott's weaving in and out of the trees, obviously having fun again.

The term all-terrain bicycle takes on new meaning as we dart at will through the trees. We ride wherever we like, picking our line based on ice coverage. Hanging over our rear wheels, we hoot and holler. The fatigue of the climb has been replaced by the adrenaline rush of descent. At the bottom we look at each other and can say no more than "Wow!" We know this experience will make for great stories for years to come.

What keeps me addicted to fear? When I'm at the edge I feel more focused, of a single purpose, the background noise in my head silenced. This is the kind of stuff that makes people question your sanity, the kind of thing that you can't tell Mom about. But to me it's a major accomplishment; it sets it apart from everyday experience and provides life with landmarks, with reference points that highlight our capabilities.

Safely back in the truck, Scott begins to realize what we've just accomplished. He's alternating between genuine awe and disbelief at the stupidity of it. I realize that it could go either way. But over dinner with friends he re-counts the day with animated enthusiasm. I know he's been won over.

In the midst of the ride, what we were doing seemed foolish—an irresponsible journey motivated by some Ramboesque need to prove ourselves. Now that we're back, it seems a conquest, a noble excursion into the wilderness, charting new territory. In reality, though, I suspect this day falls somewhere in the middle, a wildly fun and sometimes scary journey into the realm of expanded experience and reformed perceptions of the capabilities of rider and bicycle.

8

. . . . .

IT'S NOT EASY BEING GREEN

Exploring and Protecting the Natural Environment

Whenever I'm out on a trail with a class, I always point out bear turds. At first, most of my students look at me, look at each other, and look very worried. Look closely, I tell them. If it's early season, turds are fibrous—they look like there's a lot of hair in them—because bears eat a lot of grasses at that time. Later on, when bears eat mostly berries (they love raspberries), their turds become light and fluffy, sort of like a raspberry mousse. Later still, when the woods near Mount Snow explode with wild cherries, the bear crap gets full of cherry pits.

Once the class begins to understand where I'm going, their revulsion turns to curiosity, as mine did when I started. The point is that mountain biking lets you appreciate nature in a whole new way if you allow it to. You can develop rapport with your biome, your natural neighborhood. You can say things like, "Oh, the bears are eating cherries now."

By doing so, biking becomes more than just biking; it becomes a multidimensional experi-ence. It's not just about biking; it's about where the bike is taking you. The bike becomes more than just a bike; it is a vehicle that opens up your surroundings. It becomes a means to an end, not the end itself.

Mountain biking gives me more opportuni-ties to do all the things I did as a kid. Growing up in Vermont and Connecticut, I was fortu-nate enough to have a very early relationship with the outdoors. I climbed trees constantly; everyone told me I'd grow up to be a park ranger. By age twelve, I was reading, and relat-ing to, Thoreau. You might remember the se-quence in *Walden* where he walks out to the pond and submerges himself until the water is at eye level, just so he can see what it's like be-ing a frog. I read it—then ran out and did it.

It's never too late to develop that kind of bond with the environment. Even if you're a lifelong urban dweller, all it takes is an aware-ness, a desire, and a commitment to under-stand and learn more about what's around you. It's really as simple as taking a long ride and looking around in a different frame of mind. An appreciation of how precious and small our planet is will come almost naturally. Think of mountain biking as your vehicle to that relationship with the planet. It can take you fishing, or bird-watching, or rock climbing. If you open yourself to it, it truly offers unlimited access.

Nature books called field guides can help get you started. They're a terrific way to combine mountain biking with nature interests. Any bookstore should carry field guides to fish or birds or plants. The books can bring another dimension to the nature experience;

you'll realize that's not just some weed sticking out of the ground, it's a particular kind of flower. If you want to get into wild food, there are guides for that, too. Don't think of the environment as something exotic or *other*. It's right outside your door.

In high school I wrote an essay on animal intelligence and how humans, with amazing arrogance, have always separated themselves from animals and the natural world. Years ago, I wrote, the definition of a human being was "one who uses tools"—until chimps started doing it, too. Of course, there's a dividing line between the human psyche and an animal's brain. But my argument was that it wasn't an

Nature is at your fingertips . . . if you know where to look.

issue of separation but of *degree*. The traditional Western concept of nature is adversarial: nature is something to be conquered. But once we shed our preconceptions and understand other living things in a different way, it changes everything. My essay got an A, by the way.

Taking advantage of the outdoors has also made me realize how much society has influenced my perception of my surroundings. Not long after I started riding, I began seeing two points of view about the world. One posits our "civilized" way of life as the center, with streets, stores, and roads as the primary way of life. The woods are a sideshow attraction seen through a windshield. But there's another reality when you're high on a mountain, deep in the woods, peering down a tangle of roads. You realize a piece of your life is missing. Once you start riding, you notice that "developed" areas are just small strips of buildings and stores within a huge expanse of undeveloped land. That's where the mountain biking perspective comes in.

Our society is very automobile-oriented. You have to force yourself to realize you can do and see things on a bike, on your own. Once you do, the extent of human impact becomes clear. There are signs of us everywhere, even in the deep woods. And you learn to appreciate what's left. You get a balanced perspective you'd never gain looking through a windshield.

If more people could only develop that intimate sense of their environment and their biome—their natural neighborhood—we would have a much better chance of preserving our planet. And we need it. For reasons too compli-

cated to address here, I believe we're witnessing the end of the natural world. I want to look at it all before it's gone. In a modern consumer society, we're consuming the world itself. The more strip malls we build, the more roads we pave, the more we use up the planet. The way development works, land gets used for thirty years, gets old and run down, and gets left behind. We should encourage redevelopment instead of new development.

It's easy to ride your bike and assume everything's going to be there tomorrow. But things are eroding. It's not just our fault; one of the biggest problems has been the polarization of people who potentially could fight on the same sides of the issues. Environmental groups, developers, and, yes, mountain bikers are very territorial and tend to see issues in black and white. All the relationships are adversarial right now, and it hurts everyone. People battling these issues get so caught up in their own agendas that they lose sight of what they really want to accomplish.

Environmental issues are everyone's issues. From a little urban park to spectacular sights like Slick Rock, everything is precious. Start thinking of environmental issues at their most local, grassroots level. In addition to IMBA or the National Off-Road Bicycle Association (NORBA), join an organization that's *not* a mountain biking organization, such as the Sierra Club. Infiltrate! If enough mountain bikers join, these groups will have to change their politics. This isn't so we can become bomb-throwers; we'd probably agree on 99 percent of the issues, anyway. It's just to bring them our perspective.

Maybe I'm selfish about the environment,

Mountain biking offers a view of the world from a different perspective.

too. I'd hate to see mountain biking become like downhill skiing, which has developed into a totally localized, Disneyesque experience. Alpine skiing was once an individual sport. Now it's a sport of fur and groomed trails. Once you get into such a controlled environment, you lose the sense of connectedness to nature. Too many man-made accoutrements mar the quiet be

With mountain biking, you're still riding directly on the planet. Mountain biking is based on the *least* amount of construction to make a trail. Trails, once constructed, are like riding on pavement. At the same time, bikers bear a tremendous responsibility to the environment wherever they ride, and there are guidelines

The future of mountain biking?

everyone should follow to protect our natural neighborhoods. Thoughtless actions can have tremendous repercussions. As a guiding principle, riders should keep an old tenet in mind: never leave behind anything but tire tracks. And even tracks may be too much sometimes.

As mountain biking's popularity soars, advocacy groups like the Sierra Club keep singling out the sport as particularly harmful to the environment. They're wrong. Sure, irresponsible mountain biking can screw things up. But so can irresponsible hiking or golfing or fishing. Other sports just enjoy a different image. Most people perceive hikers as fervent environmentalists, while the same folks see mountain bikers as kooky yahoos out for a wild time.

In reality, the U.S. government is not being responsible. Commercial loggers do more damage in a second than an army of mountain bikers could inflict in a year. But business is powerful, and mountain bikers are scapegoats. I'd bet that if mountain bikers paid $100 each time they rode a trail, we'd suddenly see trails opening up everywhere. In fact, as a group, mountain bikers are extremely conscious of the environment and of green issues in general. Just look at the demographics: many mountain bikers are young, educated professionals for whom green thinking has become a way of life. Unfortunately, we have an image problem, and it's up to us to correct it:

1. Pick up litter. Even if you see garbage that some careless jerk tossed aside, take it and dispose of it in a proper place. You'll feel good, the trail will look good, and nature will smile upon you.

2. Never ride in restricted areas. I know this repeats one of the safety guidelines, but I can't stress enough the danger of riding in posted areas, restricted land, private property, closed areas in national forests, or wildlife preserves.

3. Avoid crossing private property when you can. You shouldn't assume a trail or an area is open for riding just because it's there. Someone built a putting green right near one of the mountain bike trails near Mount Snow. Riding over it—and trespassing in general— just upsets nonbikers and exacerbates negative perceptions. Private property remains a gray area. According to Vermont law, land has to be posted "no trespassing." But if there's no sign, it doesn't mean the property owner wants you biking across his or her lawn.

4. When riding through mud, swamp, or marshland, don't try to rip through it; walk your bike through. Wetlands are endangered, and bike tires tend to tear them up. This can lead to erosion problems from silt.

5. Since riding through streams can hurt or even kill fauna, avoid it. In Vermont and much of New England, we have three classifications for streams: Pristine, Class A, and Class B. If you pedal through a Pristine stream, there's a good chance you'll harm trout and other fish living and spawning there. Keep in mind, too, that if rain turns streambanks to mud, riding through them can create ruts. Water, in turn, flows down the ruts, which leaves silt in the stream, which also harms fish.

Every one of us represents the sport as a whole. The key is to know what's out there. Get a book about wildlife in your area, learn to identify different animals and plants. It gives you a much deeper understanding of the land you share with them. And once you gain that understanding, the land's value becomes much more apparent.

MOUNTAIN BIKE CLUBS

Throughout the book, I've emphasized the psychic and emotional benefits that each individual can reap from meeting the challenges that mountain biking offers. However powerful those personal rewards may be, don't overlook the joy and gratification you can get from entering and embracing a new community of like-minded riders. I can't overemphasize the importance of clubs as a vehicle for environmental networking. That's how every group—snowmobilers, skiers, road bikers—got where it is today as far as terrain and trails.

If you're new to the sport, you'll appreciate the group situation—sharing skill pointers, swapping dirt about trails. Even experienced bikers will find clubs can help get you out of a rut by offering different perspectives. You'll also gain a whole new social scene. I know at least one happy marriage that started as an innocent bike club acquaintance. Maybe bike trails will become to the 1990s what gyms were to the 1980s.

If clubs haven't materialized where you live, put an ad in the *NORBA News* or post a notice at your local bike store. Let mountain bikers in your area know you want to start a Saturday afternoon bike ride, or whatever. Many shops organize weekly rides, which could form the nucleus of a club.

Group riding can intimidate some first-timers, but don't let it turn you off biking clubs. Practicing at home can make you feel more comfortable—in the beginning, I spent three months biking alone until I thought I looked good. Self-consciousness is really misplaced in this sport, so relax and take the Zen approach instead: let go of ego and focus inward on your own experience. You'll realize people don't judge you the way you think they do; they're busy focusing inward themselves. In any case, falling, flipping over, and looking stupid come with the territory, so you may as well have fun.

Along with everything they offer, clubs have obligations, not only to riders but to their communities. By working to promote responsible riding, clubs can help educate the nonbiking public and change perceptions of the sport (some still see it as *A Clockwork Orange* with pedals). Even more important, clubs should enlighten members about environmental concerns. Think about sponsoring a "green-up" day on a local trail and alert the press, for example. On top of a good deed for the environment, you'll generate terrific PR for the sport. If enough clubs around the country did valuable, visible work, attitudes toward mountain biking would change. Like politics, it's all grassroots. Start from the bottom and grow.

IMBA is an example of how that kind of organization can accomplish great things. I think the group's charter can inspire riders to help take mountain biking into the future, and I've reprinted it here. I urge you to join IMBA and support it with your money, your ideas, and your time.

THE MISSION OF IMBA (Reprinted courtesy of IMBA)

IMBA's mission is to promote mountain bicycling opportunities through environmentally and socially responsible use of the land. IMBA's Board of Directors believes that mountain bicycling is becoming a leading use of trail networks in the U.S. and much of the world. It is critical that the mountain bicycling community be represented at all levels of recreational public land management.

IMBA further believes that as mountain bicycling continues to gain legitimacy as a form of outdoor recreation, nature appreciation, and transportation, it will earn greater acceptance in the mainstream environmental community.

For mountain bicyclists to merit this acceptance, they must ride with care for the environment and other trail users. The cycling industry must promote this attitude and reflect it in advertising.

IMBA must continue to promote responsible riding through education. Furthermore, IMBA must strongly advocate land preservation policies. IMBA fosters cooperative relationships with all users of all types of trails.

A VISION FOR MOUNTAIN BIKING'S FUTURE . . . AND HOW YOU CAN HELP

More people. Less open space. Recreational management budgets dwindle as cities, states, and federal agencies get caught in the fiscal crunch. Meanwhile, participation increases in all forms of outdoor recreation, particularly mountain biking.

Put all these factors together and it's easy to understand why trail pressures have mounted, and why crowded paths are contributing to trail-user tension and heightened concerns about environmental protection.

The International Mountain Bicycling Association was formed in 1988 to address these concerns. We educate mountain bikers and others trail users (such as hikers and horseback riders) in the techniques of responsible trail use. We support local cycling clubs in their efforts to maintain trails and coordinate volunteer patrols. We work with land managers to develop educational materials and management strategies that keep trail-user relations harmonious and trails in good condition. We give recreational mountain biking a unified, forward-looking voice that helps the sport develop in a sensible manner. In short, IMBA's work keeps existing trails open to cycling use and helps create new trail-riding opportunities.

THE MISSION OF IMBA (cont'd)

IMBA has a 20-20-20 vision for the future of mountain biking that involves each and every off-road cyclist. The first 20 is $20 to join your local mountain bike club, because all mountain bikers need to be involved with their local trails. The second 20 is $20 to join IMBA and become part of mountain biking's indispensable, broad-based movement. The final 20 is 20 hours per year for trails—maybe three volunteer days that can be spent on trail maintenance, trash removal at a trailhead, attending public hearings, or perhaps contributing to the production of a local club newsletter.

Mountain biking on public land is a privilege. It's a wonderful activity that is sustainable only if each and every one of us who enjoys the sport gives something back. The process is simple, and almost guaranteed to work: it's IMBA's 20-20-20 vision.

IMBA RULES OF THE TRAIL

Thousands of miles of dirt trails have been closed to mountain bicyclists. The irresponsible riding habits of a few riders have been a factor. Do your part to maintain trail access by observing the following rules of the trail, formulated by the International Mountain Bicycling Association (IMBA). IMBA's mission is to promote environmentally sound and socially responsible mountain biking.

1. **Ride on open trails only.** Respect trail and road closures (ask if not sure), avoid possible trespass on private land, obtain permits and authorization as may be required. Federal and state wilderness areas are closed to cycling. The way you ride will influence trail management decisions and policies.
2. **Leave no trace.** Be sensitive to the dirt beneath you. Even on open (legal) trails, you should not ride under conditions where you will leave evidence of your passing, such as on certain soils after a rain. Recognize different types of soils and trail construction; practice low-impact cycling. This also means staying on existing trails and not creating any new ones. Be sure to pack out at least as much as you pack in.
3. **Control your bicycle!** Inattention for even a second can cause problems. Obey all bicycle speed regulations and recommendations.

(continued)

4. **Always yield trail.** Make known your approach well in advance. A friendly greeting (or bell) is considerate and works well; don't startle others. Show your respect when passing by slowing to a walking pace or even stopping. Anticipate other trail users around corners or in blind spots.

5. **Never spook animals.** All animals are startled by an unannounced approach, a sudden movement, or a loud noise. This can be dangerous for you, others, and the animals. Give animals extra room and time to adjust to you. When passing horses use special

THE MISSION OF IMBA (cont'd)

care and follow directions from the horseback riders (ask if uncertain). Running cattle and disturbing wildlife is a serious offense. Leave gates as you found them, or as marked.

6. **Plan ahead.** Know your equipment, your ability, and the area in which you are riding—and prepare accordingly. Be self-sufficient at all times, keep your equipment in good repair, and carry necessary supplies for changes in weather or other conditions. A well-executed trip is a satisfaction to you and not a burden or offense to others. Always wear a helmet.

HOW TO PREVENT TRAIL CLOSURES

PREVENTION IS BEST

Diffuse the buildup of pressures over potential closures before the crisis stage is reached. Face the issue squarely and plan appropriate early response.

1. Start weekend patrols to warn irresponsible riders that they are hurting everyone.
2. Start a safe and responsible mountain bike riding program (with shops, clubs, or schools).
3. Have local bicycle dealers distribute IMBA's Rules of the Trail and explain to their customers why trail etiquette matters.
4. Get involved with land trail management.
5. Develop a long-term reputation for caring about the environment.
6. Foster the idea that dirt trails are not necessarily a public right of way for bikes; riding on dirt is a privilege.
7. Learn who controls the dirt access where you ride, and volunteer with groups to do trail maintenance.

RESPECT OTHER TRAIL USERS

1. Show a maximum of trail courtesy and respect to all trail users. We're all members of the trail family enjoying the quiet and natural beauty of the backcountry. We must learn to share.

(continued)

2. Take the time to set a good example. Stop, dismount, and talk with other trail users. Our motivations are no different than those of other users regardless of mode of travel.

3. Show concern for a clean, quiet backcountry experience. Keep trails as natural as possible.

4. Show that you understand other trail users' fears, needs, and desires.

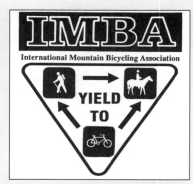

IMBA's Multiple-Use Trail Guidelines

ORGANIZE!!

1. Get a group together to further your interests and establish regular meeting times and places.

2. Develop a consensus on appropriate places to ride in the area and what is best for all concerned.

3. Communicate your concerns to other user groups and land managers. Learn about and use the political process.

4. Develop appropriate education/training programs to increase public awareness and support.

5. Adopt a trail and do other volunteer work.

6. Support IMBA and other conservation organizations. Find out what is working in other areas to provide or continue land access.

7. Don't become discouraged or bitter; democracy is sometimes slow, but persistence and a cooperative attitude will eventually pay off.

8. Develop ways to share and maintain scarce resources. Show you care by actions as well as words.

IN CASE OF IMMINENT CRISIS . . .

1. Identify decision makers who will decide the outcome of the issue. Find out where and when public hearings will be. Develop a plan and work with it. Take action!

2. Establish criteria for decisions:
   a. If public safety is the problem, push for educational barricades and safety patrols.
   b. If user input is wanted, do an analysis of trail users.

THE MISSION OF IMBA (cont'd)

    c. If affected voters must be mobilized, circulate a petition and begin a letter-writing campaign.

    d. If there is a broad base of trail users, form a coalition with other user-groups who help in trail maintenance. Volunteer together for projects.

3. Ask decision makers if you and others can present oral and written testimony. If necessary, ask for a delay in hearings to gain time to take actions above.

4. Mobilize your groups or organization. Hold meetings, attend hearings, provide information, etc.

5. Get those with an economic interest to back you: bike shops, resorts, tourist groups, newspapers, local businesses, etc. Let IMBA and other groups know what is happening.

6. Show respect and develop a responsible reputation. Learn from the process so that if you don't get what you want the first time, you will be better prepared in the future.

The Sierra Club, the oldest and most influential environmental advocacy group in the United States, has also been one of the most outspoken critics of mountain biking on public lands. In 1988, the Sierra Club adopted a highly restrictive policy on mountain biking. The policy equated the use of mountain bikes with that of motorized off-road vehicles.

For the record, the Sierra Club is a California-based, member-supported nonprofit corporation with an annual budget of $39 million and 550,000 members nationally. The bulk of its members and chapters are in California and the West. The organization's main goal is to promote conservation of the natural environment by influencing public policy decisions—legislative, administrative, legal, and electoral.

Its main focus is federal and regional legislation; it works closely with members of Congress on grassroots activism.

In April 1994, after years of work on both sides, IMBA and the Sierra Club signed a historic agreement on mountain biking and land use. The Park City Summit Agreement, as it's known, opened the doors for a dialogue where none existed before. These are the main points of that agreement:

The Sierra Club and the International Mountain Bicycling Association agree to the following principles:

    1. To work for Wilderness, park and open space protection;

2. *Mountain biking is a legitimate form of recreation and transportation on trails, including single track, when and where it is practiced in an environmentally sound and socially responsible manner;*

3. *Not all non-wilderness trails should be opened to bicycle use;*

4. *To create joint projects to educate all non-motorized trail users;*

5. *To encourage communication between local mountain bicycle groups and Sierra Club entities.*

Mark Bettinger, avid mountain biker and environmentalist, was the Sierra Club's chief architect of the Park City agreement. As Northeast regional associate representative, he supervises activities from Pennsylvania to Maine out of his office in Saratoga Springs, New York. More than 100,000 Sierra Club members live in Mark's territory alone.

Before joining the Sierra Club, he led the life of what he calls "an itinerant political and environmental organizer. I'd go from campaign to campaign and in between do environmental organizing." He's worked for the National Clean Air Coalition and the National Audubon Society, the National Wildlife Federation, and the League of Conservation Voters. He also worked on the Mondale campaign and state legislative races in Florida. He joined the Sierra Club in 1990.

Bettinger's leadership is a shining example of how mountain bikers and environmental activists can unite to further their common causes. Over coffee in his office, we talked about his involvement in both environmental-

ism and mountain biking, and how he bridges two seemingly incompatible worlds.

DK: When did the Sierra Club first become aware of mountain biking? When did it start reacting to the sport?

MB: The Sierra Club started the process in 1985 by including mountain bikes in its off-road motorized vehicle policy. The Sierra Club has had a long history of opposing unrestricted motorized vehicle use on public lands. The controversy surrounding the use of mountain bikes started in the San Francisco Bay area, where there are several Sierra Club chapters. Marin County and Mount Tamalpais [the birthplace of mountain biking and a continuing trail access hotspot] are nearby. There were some pretty serious conflicts with other trail users early on, and that influenced, and continues to influence, the overall outlook of the Sierra Club on mountain bikes.

DK: So the group didn't initially single out mountain biking as a problem?

MB: The policy lumped bicycle, or nonmotorized, mechanized vehicles in with motorized vehicles. They did make some slight distinction, but for the most part considered bicycles to have the same impacts as motorized vehicles.

DK: Did the policy distinguish among wilderness areas, national forest lands, and Bureau of Land Management lands, or privately held lands?

MB: The Sierra Club's mountain bike policy stated, and continues to state, that wilderness should remain off-limits. On other public lands, the policy is that trails are closed until they are studied and deemed appropriate for mountain bike use. Wilderness areas and public lands are the Sierra Club's meat and potatoes, bread and butter. That's what we're about—wilderness protection, not only protection from industry but also for the philosophical and spiritual benefits of preserving wilderness.

DK: What was the impetus for the recent positive changes in mountain bike policy?

MB: I think that a lot of people in leadership saw the Sierra Club getting some bad press. We were looking kind of silly at a time, in the early 1990s, when the environmental movement was taking a huge beating. An article on the front page of the *Wall Street Journal* in 1991 or 1992 described how the Sierra Club opposed mountain bikes—except a Sierra Club magazine survey revealed that half the group's members owned mountain bikes. The leadership wanted to make it clear that we are not antibicycle. We just want to protect certain areas and make sure those trails are there for everyone to use.

The other thing that helped to change things, I think, was that I came on staff, and out of my personal interest as a mountain biker, I started paying attention to different land access problems. Sierra Club staffers in San Francisco learned I was interested and asked me to look into starting a dialogue with the various Bay Area biking groups. I was already an IMBA member, so I just started calling up people like [IMBA founding member] Jim Hasenhouer and it grew from there.

DK: What does the new policy state and what effect do you think it will have in the real world of mountain biking?

MB: The original policy made it seem that mountain bikes were bad. The new policy suggests that mountain bikes are legitimate, but you need to look at whether particular trails are appropriate, and what management techniques need to be used, to make sure there is no environmental damage or public safety problem. In the real world, the change in policy is going to, and has already in a couple of instances, make it so that sides that were antagonistic can at least talk to each other.

After the Park City Summit Agreement, the Sierra Club Board of Directors detached the mountain bike policy from the off-road motorized vehicle policy and made a separate off-road use of bicycles policy. The new statement retains the same wording of the original policy statement in which the Sierra Club supports wilderness areas and the exclusion of mechanized vehicles in wilderness areas. Trails should be opened on other public lands only when there's been appropriate study done. But the thing that we were able to change, and have changed, is what's called the Background Statement, which is the justification of the policy and the guidelines for implementation. The five points of the Park City Agreement state, among other things, that while mountain biking should not be allowed in wilderness areas, it is a legitimate form of recreation and should be recognized as such. Also agreed was that not all nonwilderness trails should be open to bicycles.

Seattle is a clear success that came out of this. The process started in the beginning of this year with a couple of meetings to talk about the Juniper Ridge and Dark Divide trails, which have been up for study by the Sierra Club for a long time. Motorcycle groups and mountain bikers wanted access. The mountain bikers were trying to decide to which side they would go—the motorcyclists or the Sierra Club. We started a dialogue with the mountain bikers; it went poorly the first couple of times, but recently we agreed to work together to get some mountain bike and multiple-use trails opened in the Seattle area.

DK: Do you think it's appropriate for the Sierra Club to advocate mountain bike use?

MB: We need to make sure that there are mountain biking opportunities so that the forest manager doesn't limit access in such a way that it's concentrated. When you severely restrict trail use to a small area—whether it's mountain biking or hiking—you concentrate the impact of that use so, of course, there's going to be damage. You should be able to disperse the use so that you don't have the environmental impact from having so many bicycles on one trail every day.

DK: Some mountain bikers have told me they sense real hostility from nonbikers. Where do you think it comes from?

MB: Lack of open space, the development pressures around metropolitan areas, and at the same time the budgetary problems of the local, state, and federal land managers. Many have less and less money each year for doing trail maintenance. Other people may say the problem is the wild, wacko, radical kids that run down little old ladies and kill dogs. I think

that's missing the point. And I think someone from the Utah chapter of the Sierra Club described it best: "Mountain biking right now is about where hiking was twenty years ago. When you read a twenty- or twenty-five-year-old hiking book, it talks about going into the woods and cutting down pine boughs to sleep on every night. Well, you just don't do that anymore."

You also don't go and cut firewood anymore in most areas, so hiking and backpacking have matured in that way. With joint educational efforts by groups like the Sierra Club, IMBA, NORBA, and members of the bicycle industry, it should be possible to reach mountain bikers so that the bikers just getting into the sport now, as well as those who have been doing it for a while, understand that, just like the hikers had to learn not to cut pine boughs, when it's pouring rain, you don't go riding on a trail that collects water. Instead, ride the road for a day.

DK: Should mountain bikers join the Sierra Club?

MB: Us or any sort of organization that has the philosophy to get out there and fight for a sound environmental policy and for the conservation and acquisition of open space. The real key is to get involved, and one way to do it is through the established organizations.

DK: Should bikers note on membership applications that they're mountain bikers?

MB: It always helps to let organizations know where your interests lie. Mountain bikers in particular need to get out there and be active in already-established organizations, to dispel the perception that mountain bikers don't care about other trail users, about the resource itself, or about the environment. The more people who get out there to change that perception, the better it's going to be for mountain biking as a whole.

DK: What concessions would you make to groups who oppose mountain biking?

MB: I think the thing that mountain bikers really need to accept is that there are trails that were built as hiking trails. Even for hiking, many were not built to proper standards, so that when you put the increased use of a mountain bike on it, it's going to cause damage. As much as I hate to admit it, mountain bikes do, in those instances, increase erosion. Instead of carrying the bike over an obstacle, or learning the skills necessary to go over an obstacle, bikers widen the trail by riding off the trail and around the obstacle. People who have been hiking on these trails for years see the result and recognize it as environmental damage. It's this interaction with longtime trail users that tends to ignite potentially hot situations.

There are inconsiderate horseback riders, motorcycle riders, and hikers, and there are inconsiderate mountain bikers. If mountain bikers don't stop or say hello, or come around a blind corner at speed, they are going to scare the hell out of hikers. If it's near a city, the third time it's happened in a day, and the hikers have kids with them, they are going to be pissed. People need to be considerate of other users.

DK: What personal advice do you have to help the average mountain biker be more trail friendly?

MB: I think the most important thing is to be a good ambassador anytime you ride. If everybody who rode a mountain bike was a considerate trail user, it may be an oversimplification, but it would make my job of bringing the two sides together a lot easier. When you're out on the trail, stop and pick up trash, even if it's not yours, and make the trail better for all users. Always stop and say hello to others. Instead of riding on the trail it takes you five minutes to get to, plan to ride the road for forty-five minutes before you get to the woods, to disperse the use as much as you can.

Mountain bikers also need to consider where they are riding. If they are riding for a nice evening in the city park in the middle of town, then certainly they don't do their training, their high-speed cornering, their downhill skills in a city park. The rider needs to be aware of where he is riding and where to ride at speed. Take advantage of places like rock quarries where no one else goes—train at one of those abandoned places that are already torn up by motorized vehicles to try the wild and crazy stuff. Go where you are not likely to see hikers or other trail users. It's a tough question, I'm not sure I really know the answer to that.

I look at my experience where I've ridden. Whether it's been where I used to live in the D.C. area, or here in Saratoga. There are places right here in town where you can do your training, and there are times when it's so crowded with Sunday riders that you don't. There are other places to go.

DK: Last question. How do you see the future of the sport? Let's say ten years from now, where do you think mountain biking is going to be?

MB: I think it's going to be more legitimate. It's going to go the way of the snowboarders who are not quite the outlaws that they were ten years ago, or five years ago. My hope is that things like the Park City Agreement will prevent trail users from becoming even more factionalized—everyone has to have this trail or that trail. I think we're well under way to achieving that. Right now is the critical time to make sure that bicycles don't go the way of motorized vehicles, because they are *not* motorized vehicles. They don't do the same resource damage. My hope is that mountain bikes don't end up being limited to ski resorts in the summer. Ten years from now mountain biking is going to be a sport that continues to have a whole range of people riding—thirteen on up to fifty and beyond.

But now is a critical time. It's going to take a lot of effort. Unfortunately, it's incumbent on the bicycles, the people who ride them, the manufacturers, and the publishing industry to be good citizens, but not roll over. To move the whole agenda away from "this is mine, get off my trail" to "there are more and more people who want to get outdoors and recreate, and we need to provide the space and the budget to make it so people can get out there." And the more people get out in the woods, to appreciate what we have, the more people are going to go back and advocate for preservation. This is the way it all started a hundred years ago—taking people out in the woods to see what it's all about.

Whenever I travel I sniff out the mountain biking spots. Back in 1983, I was in South Florida, visiting a friend's parents. It was my first time in that part of the country, and my senses were assailed by the concrete and lack of natural spaces. Sure, the beaches were ok, and if I stood with my face to the breeze and my eye on the ocean, I almost felt I was the only one there. But one look at the surroundings dissolved my reverie. Everything was either human or created by humans. I'd never seen a place so totally made over by the human race. I found myself wondering what it might have been like before people got there.

The answer: Everglades National Park. While far from untouched—water that once flowed into the park is now diverted for human use; agricultural runoff pollutes the water with excess nutrients and chokes it with exotic weeds—the park is an oasis in a land changed beyond recognition by human beings.

While in Florida I spent much of my time windsurfing. I used my mountain bike only to make my way around town. It hadn't occurred to me there might be suitable off-road terrain. I'd heard of a place called Flamingo, in the park at the extreme southern tip of the Florida peninsula, where the park service rented cabins on Florida Bay, the body of water between the mainland and the Florida Keys. It sounded like a perfect place to sail—and miles from the nearest condo. I packed my sailing equipment, threw my bike on top of my truck, and headed south from Hollywood.

Soon after checking in to the cabin, I looked out over the turquoise waters of Florida Bay. The wind was whipping the water into a soft blue foam. It was the perfect wind for me, about 15 knots—not too strong, nice and steady, and on-shore. Only one thing was missing: other windsurfers. There were a couple of pleasure boats on the water, but not one board sailor. I headed out to the parking lot that fronted on the water and saw a park ranger.

"How's the sailing here?" I pointed to the gear on the roof of my car.

"I bet it would be pretty good," he replied, and added, as an afterthought, "Have to watch out for the sharks, though." The third *Jaws* sequel had just come out. I imagined my arms and legs being severed from my body in a sea boiling red with blood.

"What about the lakes?" I asked, determined not to be deterred. The park is dotted with lakes, some of them quite large.

"Oh I bet they'd be good, too," he said, then paused. I waited for what I knew was coming. "Have to watch out for the 'gators though, 'specially this time of year." There's nothing worse than windsurfing when you're afraid to fall in the water. It's one of those self-fulfilling prophecies; the more you think about falling, the more likely it is you will.

I started thinking about off-road riding instead. There are miles of trails along the many canals that were built through the swamp over the years. I'd also read about fire roads that crisscross the pinelands and the coastal plain.

"Can I ride my bike on the trails?" I asked. Hope springs eternal.

"I don't think you could ride a bike on the trails," the ranger said helpfully.

"You mean I can't, or I'm not allowed?"

He raised an eyebrow. "You can try if you wanna but I don't know. . . ."

That was all I wanted to hear. I spent the next week exploring hundreds of incredible miles of single track in the Everglades.

Before you start planning your next mountain biking vacation in the Sunshine State, keep two things in mind: first, it's illegal to ride your bike on most of the trails now. Remember, I was there in 1983, the dark ages. Second, there are nasty things out in the mangrove swamps, from poisonous snakes and spiders to alligators and who knows what else. And then there's the coral and the mosquitoes. I know firsthand why coral, mountain biking, and mosquitoes don't mix.

Back in 1983, when I was younger (twenty-eight) and considerably more foolish (unquantifiable), I did some pretty silly stuff. First, you couldn't get mountain bike pumps (at least I couldn't) to fit on your frame; all that was available were road bike pumps. If you've ever tried to pump up a 2½-inch-wide mountain bike tire with a road pump you know that you'll probably have grandchildren before you're done. So you know what I did? I attached a floor pump to my top tube with a bungee cord. This was well before the days of lightweight accessories—it was, as a matter of fact, before the days of just about anything. There were no mountain bike shoes, special clothing, magazines, no NORBA and IMBA. You name it, I didn't have it. Except, of course, for the bike.

So there I was, ten miles out into the swamp, riding as fast as I could to keep ahead of the mosquitoes, weighed down with a thirty-five-pound bike, a ten-pound pump, and every tool known to mankind, thinking I'm ready for anything. I wasn't.

I didn't count on coral—coral rock, that is—the foundation of the Florida peninsula. Coral is sharp—sharp enough that it tore a tire and gave me a flat within ten minutes of my ride. Undaunted by the swarming bugs I used my one and only spare tube (the nearest new tube was ninety miles away in Miami at a beach cruiser rental shop) and continued on my way.

I found an incredible trail, smooth and fast, lined with man-size flowering yuccas and spiders as big as your fist, spinning their webs in the spiny leaves. The trail led out of the mangrove swamp and onto the coastal plain, a treeless expanse of grass looking not so much like Florida as the Serengeti Plain. I expected to see hippos and giraffes. I was truly stunned by my surroundings. It didn't seem possible that I was in Florida, home of high-rise beach hotels and 7-Elevens on every corner.

My rapture was broken by a hideous sound. At first I thought I'd run over a snake and it was hissing a prebite warning at me. No such luck. It was my front tire exhaling its dying breath. No problem, I told myself. Though I'd used my last tube, I had a patch kit. I'd just patch the tire and go on my way.

Not. When I got my patch kit out I discovered that the glue, unused since the previous season, had turned to stone. No amount of squeezing would produce even a drop of usable adhesive. I was choking on mosquitoes, trying to tune out their deafening drone. My mind started racing. I had repellent, but on a sweaty, half-naked Yankee, it would have been as effective as smearing honey.

So I ran. I hoisted forty-five pounds of bike and equipment on my shoulder and ran like hell. So many bugs swarmed around my eyes I could barely see. I remember an alligator lying across the trail on my way back. I didn't have time to think about what to do—I leapt over it and kept going. I stopped once, in near exhaustion, and did what any other American tourist would do in a life-threatening situation: I took a picture. I propped my camera in the crotch of a mangrove and set the timer to take a picture of me. I figured no one would believe my story, so I had to record it for posterity. I still have the photo, which I pull out occasionally so that I can relive the full extent of my foolish youth.

It took me about an hour and a half to reach the cabin, during which I had time to think about several important lessons I'd learned, which form the moral of our story. First, respect nature, because just when you think you have her figured out, she'll slap you right in the face and let you know otherwise. Second, check your tool kit on a regular basis; a little thing like dried glue can be a big bummer. Finally, and most important, incredible outdoor experiences are anywhere you are—right outside your door in the most unlikely and unexpected places. Open yourself to the possibilities and have the time of your life!

I drove all the way to Miami the next day, bought a beach cruiser shop out of tubes, and returned to my cabin to scratch my 10,000 mosquito bites and finish my adventure in the Everglades. I rode dozens of trails, got a half-dozen flats, and had the time of my life.

APPENDIX A

· · · · ·

Glossary

ATB   All-terrain bicycle.

Bars   The metal protrusions you use to steer your bike (also known as handlebars), or a place to find the perfect margarita.

Bead   The part of your tire that fits onto the rim, either wire (heavy and cheap) or Kevlar (light and expensive), or what you find in Missy Giovie's hair.

Biff   Wipe; crash; eat it; become one with the trail.

Bonk   What happens when you haven't had breakfast before your ride (running out of energy from low blood sugar), or what happens to your head when you endo without a helmet.

Bottom bracket   The bearing assembly to which your crank arms attach.

Brake pad   The rubber block that attaches to the brake cantilever arms and makes your bike stop or slow down.

Braze-on   Threaded attachment welded to the bike frame to accept the mounting of brake sets, water bottle cages, rear racks, etc.

Bunny hop   Lifting both wheels of the bike off the ground to clear an obstacle while riding.

Cadence   The rate at which the crank arms are spun while riding, measured in revolutions per minute (rpm).

Cantilever brake   The most common type of brake found on mountain bikes today. Named for the two cantilever arms that pivot on the forks (front) or seat stays (rear).

Chain rings   The gears on the front of the bike; part of the crank arm assembly.

Chain stays   The pieces of the bike frame, parallel to the chain, extending from the bottom bracket to the rear hub, comprising the base of the rear triangle of the frame.

Chain suck   A situation in which the chain gets caught between the chain rings and the chain stay, usually from worn-out chain rings or an excessively dirty chain.

Clean   The ability to negotiate a technical section of trail without dabbing.

Clipless pedal system   A shoe-pedal system in which the shoe is held in place on the pedal with a releasable cleat rather than a traditional toe clip and strap.

Cog   A single gear, usually referring to the rear gear cluster.

Components   The moving parts of a bike that are attached to the frame, such as the brakes, derailleurs, cranks, etc.

Crank arms   The metal arms to which the pedals attach.

Dab   To put a foot down to prevent a fall—humiliating but sometimes necessary.

Death grip   An overly tight grip on the handlebars caused by fear of terrain.

Derailleur   Mechanical apparatus that moves the chain from cog to cog (in the rear) or between chain rings (front), thus changing gears.

Dialed in   The blissful state of perfect harmony with the trail, handling terrain appropriately and competently.

Down tube   The part of the frame that connects the head tube and the bottom bracket.

Dropouts   The U-shaped slots that accept the wheel axle.

Endo   The act of going over the handlebars, derived from "end over end."

Face plant   A common result of an endo.

Fork   The detachable swiveling section of the frame that holds the front wheel. It looks more like a tuning fork than an eating utensil.

Freewheel/Freehub   The part of the rear gear cluster that allows the bike to coast without the pedals turning.

Freewheeling   Coasting with the pedals motionless.

Gear cluster   An assembly of gears; usually described by their configuration: "my rear cluster is a 13-30."

Get air   To go airborne.

Gnarly   An archaic teenage term for "cool" or "difficult."

Granny gear   The easiest gear combination on your bike (the one that Granny would use).

Headset   The bearing assembly that attaches the fork to the head tube.

Head tube   The short frame member that attaches the top tube to the down tube and holds the headset in place.

Hub   Assembly that holds the axle, located at the center of the wheel attached to the rim by the spokes.

Pick a line   To plan the path of the bike by anticipating approaching terrain.

Pinch flat   Flat tire caused when the tube is pinched between the rim and a hard object, usually owing to an underinflated tire.

Pump   Instrument to get air in your tube, or how to get excited about riding.

Quick release   Bolt with lever attached, for easy adjustment and removal of wheels and seat height.

Racing bike   One of those funny-looking, skinny-tired road things.

Rear triangle   The triangle formed by the chain stays, seat stays, and seat tube.

Ride the pegs   To stand on the pedals through rough terrain; I call it "building a platform."

Road bike   See RACING BIKE.

Saddle   The bike seat.

Seat post   The post that attaches your seat to the frame at the seat tube.

Seat stay   The two frame members through which the rear wheel passes that meet the chain stays at the rear dropouts.

Seat tube   The part of the frame that accepts the seat post and attaches the top tube to the bottom bracket.

Shifter   The lever that activates the derailleurs.

Single track   Narrow trail formed by two-wheeled (or two-legged) vehicles.

Slick   Mountain bike tire with no tread for lower rolling resistance, used on pavement or on Slick Rock Trail.

Snakebite   Same as PINCH FLAT, so-called because of the two fanglike punctures left by the rim.

Spin   The act of turning the pedals. See CADENCE.

Spin-out   Loss of traction in the rear tire, resulting in the wheel spinning with no forward movement of the bike, usually while climbing on loose gravel.

Stem   The piece of metal that attaches the handlebars to the headset.

Technical section   A difficult section of trail that requires specific mountain bike technique to negotiate.

Top tube   The part of the frame that attaches the head tube to the seat tube.

Trackstand   To hover motionless on your bike with both feet on the pedals.

Trials   A competitive skill-based event in which riders are rated for their ability to clean an ultradifficult section of trail.

True   The ability of a wheel to spin with no lateral wobble.

Valve stem   The point where the pump is attached to fill the tube with air; valve stems come in two types: Shraeder (standard American style, like the valve found on your car tire) or Presta (funny-looking Italian style; tall and skinny).

Wheelie   Riding a bike with the front wheel off the ground—silly looking, but a useful skill.

APPENDIX B

Resource Guide

BICYCLING ASSOCIATIONS AND ORGANIZATIONS

Adventure Cycling Association
P.O. Box 8308
Missoula, MT 59807
406-721-1776

A national membership organization dedicated to worldwide bicycle travel.

Bicycle Federation of America
1506 21st Street NW, Suite 200
Washington, DC 20036
202-463-6622

The Bicycle Federation of America serves as a clearinghouse for information on all aspects of bicycling.

International Mountain Bicycling Association (IMBA)
P.O. Box 7578
Boulder, CO 80306
303-545-9011
E-mail: IMBA@aol.com

IMBA promotes mountain biking opportunities through environmentally and socially responsible use of land. IMBA also has over 300 affiliated local clubs nationwide and a quarterly newsletter.

League of American Bicyclists
190 W. Ostend Street, Suite 120
Baltimore, MD 21230
301-539-3399

Formerly the league of American Wheelmen, the League of American Bicyclists is a national membership organization that lobbies for cyclists' rights through a combination of national advocacy and education and grassroots organizing.

National Mountain Bike Patrol (NMBP)
c/o NORBA
One Olympic Plaza
Colorado Springs, CO 80909
719-578-4717

The National Mountain Bike Patrol (NMBP) is a volunteer training program offered jointly by the NORBA and the National Ski Patrol, in conjunction with IMBA and local, state, or federal land management agencies. The purpose of the program is to provide trailside support and assistance to the mountain biking public. Volunteers are trained in outdoor emergency care, trail user etiquette (including environmental issues), and mechanical assistance.

National Off-Road Bicycle Association (NORBA)
One Olympic Plaza
Colorado Springs, CO 80909
719-578-4717

The governing body of competitive mountain biking in the United States, NORBA has over 30,000 members nationally.

Rails to Trails Conservancy
1400 16th Street NW, Suite 300
Washington, DC 20036
202-797-5400
Fax: 202-797-5411

The Rails to Trails Conservancy is an organization dedicated to the conversion of abandoned railroad rights-of-way to recreational trails.

ENVIRONMENTAL ORGANIZATIONS

Adirondack Mountain Club
P.O. Box 367
Lake Placid, NY 12946
518-523-3441

Alliance for the Wild Rockies
P.O. Box 8731
Missoula, MT 59807
406-721-3621

American Alpine Club (AAC)
710 Tenth Street, Suite 100
Golden, CO 80401
303-384-0110
Fax: 303-384-0111

Appalachian Mountain Club
202 E. 39th Street
New York, NY 10016
212-986-1430

Ecotourism Society
P.O. Box 755
North Bennington, VT 05275
802-447-2121

National Audubon Society
700 Broadway
New York, NY 10012
212-979-3000

National Wildlife Federation
1400 Sixteenth Street, NW
Washington, DC 20036
703-790-4363

The Nature Conservancy
1815 North Lynn Street
Arlington, VA 22209
703-841-5300

Outdoor Recreation Coalition of America
P.O. Box 1319
Boulder, CO 80306
303-444-3353
Fax: 303-444-3284
E-mail: orcamail@aol.com

Sierra Club
730 Polk Street
San Francisco, CA 94109
415-776-2211

Student Conservation Association (SCA)
P.O. Box 550
Charlestown, NH 03603
603-543-1700
Fax: 603-543-1828

Tread Lightly!
298 24th Street, Suite 325
Ogden, UT 84401
801-627-0077; 800-966-9900
Fax: 801-621-8633

EDUCATIONAL RESOURCES

American Heart Association (CPR Training)
122 E. 42nd Street
New York, NY 10017
212-661-5335

The national headquarters can provide the location of regional chapters that offer first-aid training, with an emphasis on CPR.

American Red Cross
National Headquarters
2025 E Street NW
Washington, DC 20006
202-737-8300

The national headquarters can provide the location of regional chapters that offer first-aid training.

National Safety Council
1121 Spring Lake Drive
Itasca, IL 60143-3201
800-621-7656

The national office can provide the location of regional safety associations that offer first-aid training.

National Ski Patrol (Outdoor Emergency Care Training)
133 S. Van Gordon, Suite 100
Lakewood, CO 80228
303-988-1111
Judy Over, National Education Director

The Outdoor Emergency Care Training programs provide comprehensive emergency care training for the nonurban setting and are the source for the care programs and materials of the National Mountain Bike Patrol.

TOUR OPERATORS BY REGION, U.S. AND FOREIGN

NORTHEAST

Back Country Excursions of Maine
Clifford Krolick, Director
RFD 2, Box 365
Limerick, ME 04048
207-625-8189

Bike the Light Fantastic
195 Goodenough Road
Brattleboro, VT 05301-8965
802-257-2612

Biking Expedition (for Teens Only)
Allyson Geary, Director
P.O. Box 547
Henniker, NH 03242
800-245-4649

Birches Resorts/Wilderness Expeditions
P.O. Box 41-MB
Rockwood, ME 04478
800-825-WILD; 800-825-9453; 207-534-7305
Fax: 207-534-8835
E-mail: WWLD@aol.com

Forest City Mountain Bike Tours
John Clark, Director
51 Melbourne Street
Portland, ME 04101
207-780-8155

Getaway Adventures
509 W. 37th Street
Wilmington, DE 19802
800-434-BIKE; 302-761-9847

Maine Wheels
RR#1 Box 3278
Norway, ME 04268
207-743-9018

SOUTHEAST

America Outdoors
P.O. Box 1348
Knoxville, TN 37901
615-524-4814
Fax: 615-525-4765
E-mail: Amoutdoors@aol.com

Backcountry Outfitters
P.O. Box 1450
Pisgah Forest, NC 28768

Camp Carolina—Home of NUMBA
(Naked Underwater Mountain Bike Association)
P.O. Box 552
Brevard, NC 28712
704-884-2414

Festivals held on Memorial Day and Labor Day annually.

Elk River Touring Center
Slaty Fork, WV 26291
304-572-3771

Pineapple Pedalers
R.R. 1, Box 15
McGaheysville, VA 22840
800-893-2516

CENTRAL STATES

Outer Edge Expeditions
45500 Pontiac Trail
Walled Lake, MI 48390
800-322-5235
Fax: 810-624-6744
E-mail: oedgeexp@aol.com

MOUNTAIN STATES

Adventure Cycling Association (formerly Bike-centennial)
150 E. Pine Street
P.O. Box 8308
Missoula, MT 59807-8308
406-721-1776

Nonprofit organization offering membership. ACA has three categories of tours: expeditions, treks, and events.

Aspen Alpine Guides
P.O. Box 659
Aspen, CO 81612
800-643-8621

Backcountry Tours
P.O. Box 4029-OL
Bozeman, MT 59772
406-586-3556
Fax: 406-586-4288

Bicycle Tour of Colorado
Kent Powell, Director
3500 S. Wadsworth #201

Lakewood, CO 80235
303-985-1180
Fax: 303-988-9568

Kaibab Mountain/Desert Bike Tours
391 South Main Street
Moab, UT 84532
800-451-1133; 801-259-7423
Fax: 801-259-6135

Mountain Bike Specialists
P.O. Box 1389-MBM
Durango, CO 81302
303-247-4066

New Mexico Mountain Bike Adventures
6 Grasshopper Road
Madrid, NM 87010
505-264-5888
Fax: 505-473-1374

Nichols Expeditions
497 North Main
Moab, UT 84532
800-648-8488; 801-259-3999
Fax: 801-259-2312
E-mail: nictrips@aol.com

Paragon Guides
P.O. Box 130
Vail, CO 81658
303-926-5299
E-mail: 75501.3353@compuserve.com

Remolino Excursions
P.O. Box 2555
Sunland, NM 88063
505-589-0519

Rim Tours
94 West, 1st North
Moab, UT 84532
800-626-7335; 801-259-5223

La Rinconada
P.O. Box 1621
Santa Fe, NM 87504-1621

505-989-3359
Fax: 505-989-3359
E-mail: La Ricon@aol.com

Roads Less Traveled
P.O. Box 8187
Longmont, CO 80501
800-488-8483; 303-678-8750
Fax: 303-678-5568

Timberline Bicycle Tours
7975 E. Harvard Ave. #J
Denver, CO 80231
303-759-3804

Trails and Rails Downhill Mountain Bike Tours
P.O. Box 217
1106 Rose Street
Georgetown, CO 80444
800-691-4FUN; 303-670-1686
Fax: 303-569-2894

WESTERN STATES

Camp Alaska Tours
P.O. Box 872247
Wasilla, AK 99687
800-376-9438

Mammoth Adventure Connection
P.O. Box 353
Mammoth Lakes, CA 93546
800-228-4947; 619-934-0606
Fax: 619-934-0700

Mountain & River Adventures
11113 Kernville Road
P.O. Box 858
Kernville, CA 93238
800-861-6553; 619-376-6553

Outland Adventures
P.O. Box 16343
Seattle, WA 98116
206-932-7012
Fax: 206-932-7012

REI Adventure Travel
P.O. Box 1938
1700 45th Street East
Sumner, WA 98390-0800
800-622-2236; 206-395-8111
Fax: 206-395-4744

Wheel Escapes
30 Liberty Ship Way #210
Sausalito, CA 94965
415-332-0218
Fax: 415-332-0417

World O' Travel
22964 Victory Boulevard
Woodland Hills, CA 91367
800-660-0828; 818-999-5250
Fax: 818-999-3964

INTERNATIONAL

Asian Pacific Adventures
826 South Sierra Bonita Avenue
Los Angeles, CA 90036
800-825-1680; 213-935-3156
Fax: 213-935-2691

Baja Montana Tours
P.O. Box 189003-118
Coronado, CA 92178-9003
800-298-8085

Mountain bike tours in Baja California, Mexico.

Elk Valley Mountain Bike Tours
P.O. Box 2560
Fernie, B.C. V0B 1M0
Canada
604-423-6871
Fax: 604-423-3773

Europeds
761 Lighthouse Avenue
Monterey, CA 93940
800-321-9552; 408-646-4920
Fax: 408-655-4501

Lost World Adventures
1189 Autumn Ridge Drive
Marietta, GA 30066
800-999-0558; 770-971-8586
Fax: 770-977-3095

Andes Mountains and Costa Rica mountain biking expeditions.

New Zealand Pedaltours
522 29th Avenue South
Seattle, WA 98144
206-323-2080
Fax: 206-727-6597

Sea to Sky Cycling Vacations
P.O. Box 1523
Whistler, BC V0N 1B0
Canada
800-336-0788

Thierry Tours
P.O. Box 8015
New York, NY 10150
800-742-3872

Mountain bike tours in France's wine country.

Government Agencies and Resources

U.S. Geological Survey
Denver, CO 80225
Reston, VA 22092

Sources for detailed topographical maps of the entire United States.

Land Management Agencies

Bureau of Land Management
Outdoor Recreation Division
1849 C Street NW, Room 204 LS
Washington, DC 20240
202-452-7794

Or contact the "recreation planner" of any BLM office.

Bureau of Land Management
Colorado State Office
2850 Youngfield
Lakewood, CO 80215
303-239-3733

National Park Service
Recreation Resources Assistance
P.O. Box 37127
Washington, DC 20013-7127
202-343-3779

U.S. Forest Service
Recreation Division
Brent Botts, National Trails Coordinator
201 14th Street, SW
Washington, DC 20250
202-205-1313

Or contact the "dispersed recreation planner" of any ranger district office.

For Trail Concerns on State Lands

Contact the state trails coordinator at the state parks administrative office in the capital city (deals with statewide trails issues on all public lands), or the local state park manager, if an individual state park is involved.

Trail User Etiquette and Environmental Concerns

International Mountain Bike Association (IMBA)
P.O. Box 7578
Boulder, CO 80306
303-545-9011
E-mail: IMBA@aol.com

IMBA promotes mountain biking opportunities through environmentally and socially responsible use of land.

Leave No Trace
National Outdoor Leadership School (NOLS)
288 Main
Lander, WY 82520
800-332-4100

Provides materials and training promoting "no trace" recreational use of public lands.

Tread Lightly!
298 24th Street, Suite 325
Ogden, UT 84401
800-966-9900

An educational program dedicated to increasing awareness on how to enjoy public and private lands while minimizing impact.

TRAIL-RELATED ORGANIZATIONS

National Trails Day
American Hiking Society
P.O. Box 20160
Washington, DC 20041-2160
703-255-9304

A nationwide day of public events celebrating trails and the volunteers who maintain them.

PERIODICALS

Adventure Cyclist Magazine
P.O. Box 8308
Missoula, MT 59807
406-721-1776
Fax: 406-721-8754

American Bicyclist
400 Skokie Boulevard #395
Northbrook, IL 60062
708-291-1117

Bicycle Guide
6420 Wilshire Boulevard
Los Angeles, CA 90048
213-782-2349

Bicycling
135 N. 6th Street
Emmaus, PA 18098
610-967-8093
Fax: 610-967-8960

Bike
33046 Calle Aviados
San Juan Capistrano, CA 92675
714-496-5922
Fax: 714-496-7849

The Bike Mag
Link House
Dingwall Avenue
Croydon CR9 2TA
England

California Bicyclist
490 2nd Street
San Francisco, CA 94107
415-546-7291
Fax: 415-546-9106

Cycle World
853 West 17th
Costa Mesa, CA 92627
714-720-5300
Fax: 714-720-7973

Cyclosource
Adventure Cycling
P.O. Box 8308
Missoula, MT 59807-8308
800-721-8719 (Sales orders, customer service, or product questions)
Fax: 800-721-8719

Earthwatch
680 Mount Auburn Street
Watertown, MA 02271
617-926-8200

Ecotraveler
7730 S.W. Mohawk Street
Tualatin, OR 97062
503-691-1955; 800-334-8152

Mountain Bike
33 E. Minor Street
Emmaus, PA 18098
215-967-5171
Fax: 215-967-8960

Mountain Bike Action
25233 Anza Drive
Valencia, CA 91355
805-295-1910
Fax: 805-295-1278

Mountain West Outdoors
2330 Syringa Road
Post Falls, ID 83854
208-773-7174

Northeast Outdoors
P.O. Box 2180
Waterbury, CT 06722-2180
203-755-0158

On-Dirt Magazine
P.O. Box 411
Woodland Hills, CA 91365
818-340-5750
Fax: 818-348-4648

Outside
400 Market Street
Santa Fe, NM 87501
505-989-7100; 800-678-1131

Sierra
730 Polk Street
San Francisco, CA 94109-7813
415-776-2211

The official publication of the Sierra Club.

Touring America
P.O. Box 6050
Mission Viejo, CA 92690
714-855-8822
Fax: 714-855-3045

Western Outdoors
3197-E Airport Loop
Costa Mesa, CA 92626
714-546-4370

MOUNTAIN BIKING BOOKS

Bicycling Magazine's Mountain Biking Skills. Rodale Press, 1990; 212-674-5151.

Covers the basics of simple maintenance and repair, riding techniques, backcountry skills, and minor medical treatment.

Fat Tire Rider: Everyone's Guide to Mountain Biking, Martha J. Kennedy et al. Vitesse Press, 1993; 802-257-5840.

Detailed information on mechanics, fitness, techniques and tricks, competition, and backcountry manners.

Mountain Bike Emergency Repair, Tim Toyoshima. The Mountaineers, 1995; 206-223-6303.

Shows how to fix just about anything on a bike, no matter where you are, no matter what you have with you.

Mountain Bike Techniques: An Illustrated Guide, Dennis Coello. Lyons & Burford, 1992; 212-620-9580.

A no-nonsense, fully illustrated guide to techniques, on-the-trail repairs, trail etiquette, and backcountry touring.

RELATED TITLES

Conflicts on Multi-Use Trails: Synthesis of the Literature and State of the Practice, Dr. Roger Moore. Federal Highway Administration, 1994; 202-366-4634.

Provides twelve principles for minimizing conflicts on multiple-use trails.

Introduction to Basic Trail Maintenance, Kurt Loheit and Frank Padilla, Jr. International Mountain Bike Association, 1994; 303-545-9011.

Detailed information on trail standards, maintenance, and volunteer involvement.

Leave No Trace Outdoor Skills and Ethics. National Outdoor Leadership School, 1992; 800-332-4100.

Informational brochure providing techniques for "no trace" recreational use of public lands.

Mountain Bikes on Public Lands: A Manager's Guide to the State of the Practice, Kit Keller. Bicycle Federation of America, 1990; 202-463-6622.

Summary of information about managing mountain bike use on public land; explores management issues and techniques and suggests possible actions.

Mountain Bike Trails: Techniques for Design, Construction and Maintenance, Michael McCoy and Mary-Alice Stoner. Adventure Cycling Association, 1992; 406-721-1776.

Addresses trail planning and layout, supplemental information for mountain bike trail guidelines, and construction and maintenance techniques.

A New Perspectives Approach in National Forest Recreation and Its Application to Mountain Bike Management, Andy Kulla. U.S. Forest Service, 1991; 406-329-3750.

Report providing a hierarchy of options for managing trail user conflicts; list of ideas of how to improve mountain bikers' image, take care of land, and reduce user conflicts.

Tread Lightly's Guide to Responsible Mountain Biking. Tread Lightly! Inc., 1995; 800-966-9900.

Brochure providing details on all aspects of backcountry biking, including trip organization, safety, rules and courtesy, environmental ethics, and an equipment checklist.

REGIONAL TRAIL GUIDES

Adventurous Traveler Bookstore
P.O. Box 577
Hinesburg, VT 05461
800-282-3963 (phone/fax USA & Canada)
802-482-3546 (phone/fax international)
E-mail: books@atbook.com
www: http//www.gorp.com/atbook.htm

The Adventurous Traveler Bookstore is a mail-order retailer specializing in outdoor recreation and adventure travel books. Their stock of 3,000 titles includes over 500 biking books and maps, covering destinations in both the United States and around the world. Free 32-page catalog.

MOUNTAIN BIKING ON THE INTERNET

NEWSGROUPS

rec.bicycles.marketplace
Buying, selling, and reviewing cycling products

rec.bicycles.misc
General discussion of cycling

rec.bicycles.off-road
Discussions of all aspects of off-road cycling

rec.bicycles.racing
Bicycle racing techniques, rules, and results

rec.bicycles.rides
Tours and training

rec.bicycles.soc
Societal issues of cycling

rec.bicycles.tech
Discussions of product design, construction, and maintenance

WORLDWIDE WEB

The Worldwide Web is a new, exciting, and constantly changing source for information about mountain biking products, tours, and destinations. The best way to surf the web for information is through a web browser using a key-word search of either *bike* or *mountain bike*. I did find one site that has dozens of useful links for mountain bikers: GORP—Great Outdoor Recreation Pages—located at http://www.gorp.com.

GORP's Attraction pages feature descriptions of most of the U.S. national parks, forests, and wilderness areas. Descriptions of the national wildlife refuges and national monuments are in process. The site contains tons of information on popular outdoor activities and topics including hiking, biking, climbing, fishing, paddle sports, skiing, caving, hang gliding, nature and wildlife, ecology, and navigation. Pages arranged by geographic location provide pointers to state or country home pages on the net that include outdoor recreation and/or travel information. Also included on GORP are listings for trips, books and maps, magazines, and nonprofit organizations pertinent to outdoor recreationists and activity travelers.

INDEX

■ ■ ■ ■ ■